Threads of Evidence

USING FORENSIC SCIENCE TO SOLVE CRIMES

HERMA SILVERSTEIN

TWENTY-FIRST CENTURY BOOKS
A Division of Henry Holt and Company • New York

*To forensic scientists, who uncover the truth
in the hope that justice will prevail*

Twenty-First Century Books
A Division of Henry Holt and Company, Inc.
115 West 18th Street
New York, NY 10011

Henry Holt® and colophon are trademarks of
Henry Holt and Company, Inc.
Publishers since 1866

Library of Congress Cataloging-in-Publication Data
Silverstein, Herma.
Threads of evidence: using forensic science to solve crimes/Herma Silverstein.
p. cm.
Includes bibliographical references and index.
Summary: Examines ways in which science helps solve crimes, using
threads of evidence such as blood, teeth, teethmarks, fingerprints,
eye prints, DNA, hairs, fibers, and corpses.
1. Forensic sciences—Juvenile literature. 2. Criminal investigation—Juvenile
literature. [1. Forensic sciences. 2. Criminal investigation.] I. Title
HV8073.S474 1996
363.2'5—dc20   96-32701
                                                                   CIP
                                                                   AC
ISBN 0-8050-4370-5
First Edition–1996

DESIGNED BY KELLY SOONG

Printed in the United States of America
All first editions are printed on acid-free paper ∞.

1   3   5   7   9   10   8   6   4   2

C O N T E N T S

INTRODUCTION

Whenever you enter a room, you carry something into that room with you. And whenever you exit a room, you leave something you brought with you behind. This is the scientific fact behind all forensic investigations.

To hide their identity, criminals may wear gloves, a face mask, or even a wet suit. Even so, some clue to the criminal's identity will be left behind and remain at the crime scene, just waiting for the police to discover it. The clue may be a criminal's fingerprint, a hair from his head, a bullet casing from a killer's gun, or a spattering of a criminal's own blood. This is what forensic investigation is all about—finding these "threads of evidence" and analyzing them to link a criminal to a crime.

There is no record of exactly when forensic science was first used in criminal investigation. Until the 1960s, the police did not fully utilize forensics, and preferred "good old detecting." They were interested mostly in evidence they could see and touch—hard evidence. These detectives would turn on bright lights at a crime scene to see the evidence better. In contrast, today's detectives may turn off the bright lights. They use alternate light sources, such as laser beams and ultraviolet or infrared lights, to find evidence. Then they conduct chemical tests on that evidence. "Gone are the days when we'd go to a crime scene and pick up whatever we could see," FBI (Federal Bureau of Investigation) special agent Dale Moreau says. "Nowadays we're more interested in evidence we can't see."[1]

The earliest recorded use of forensic medicine was to determine whether or not a death was a suicide. Simple inspection of a dead person for such reasons came to be known as an autopsy. The medical person who examined the body was named the coroner. The coroner system developed in 1194 in England. King Richard I ordered his royal justices to appoint three knights and a clerk in every county to determine whether a death was a murder or suicide. These early coroners held inquests to uncover all unnatural deaths, for which the king could collect the murderer's property. In cases of suicide, the king collected the deceased's property.

The coroner system was adopted by American colonists in the seventeenth century. By 1860, Maryland required coroners to employ physicians in the investigation of suspicious deaths. (In 1915, New York City replaced the coroner with a medical examiner system that became the model for other police departments throughout the United States.)

Forensic pathology, a branch of medicine concerned with analyzing body tissues and fluids to determine the cause of death, grew as a science from the early coroner system. In 1807, the University of Edinburgh in Scotland established a forensic science institute that had the first professional department of legal medicine. In America, the scientific status of forensic pathology was acknowledged in 1937, when Harvard Medical

School created a department of legal medicine and offered special courses, research, and educational seminars in forensics.

While Sherlock Holmes, the famous fictional detective, used a simple magnifying glass to find clues, he also used forensic techniques to analyze blood, poisons, and other evidence found at crime scenes. Sir Arthur Conan Doyle, British physician and author of the Sherlock Holmes stories, began writing his stories in the 1880s. Some historians claim Doyle foresaw the future use of scientific methods to solve crimes. Whether or not Doyle saw into the future, it is true that forensic science emerged as a significant crime-detecting tool in the late nineteenth and early twentieth centuries, shortly after the Sherlock Holmes stories were published. French professor Alexandre Lacassagne, for example, discovered that the inside of every gun is unique. Scars carved into a fired bullet could be traced to the gun that fired it. Paul Uhlenhuth, a German scientist, pioneered bloodstain identification with a test that distinguished between animal and human blood.[2]

In 1879, Frenchman Alphonse Bertillon invented a primitive method of identifying people by a photograph of the person, which became the world's first "mug shots," along with a way to identify people based on the measurements of their body parts, including height, dimension of the head, and length of the arms, legs, and feet.

In 1892, Sir Francis Galton showed that every person's fingerprints are unique to that person and do not change with age. Thus, fingerprints of criminals found at crime scenes could be saved and later used to match with fingerprints found at other crime scenes. By 1894, Scotland Yard (the detective department of the London police) included the Galton method of fingerprinting in their investigations.

In 1904, the New York City Police Department began routinely fingerprinting people they arrested. Other United States police departments quickly followed suit. By 1910, law enforcement agents in the United States were routinely taking fingerprints of suspects and filing them according to the major pattern in the print—loop, whorl, arch, or a combination of the three. In 1910, French criminologist Edmond Locard, said to be inspired by the Sherlock Holmes stories, established the world's first crime laboratory in Paris to analyze crime scene evidence. The success of Dr. Locard's lab made other criminal investigators realize the need for a scientific approach to collecting and analyzing crime scene evidence, and during the 1920s forensic laboratories were established throughout Europe.

The first American crime lab opened in Los Angeles, California, in 1923. Six years later, a second forensic laboratory opened at Northwestern University in Evanston, Illinois. But it was only after two of the most infamous crimes in American history were solved by forensic techniques that a United States federal forensic laboratory was opened.[3]

THE SACCO AND VANZETTI CASE

On April 15, 1920, a paymaster and a guard carrying a $16,000 payroll for a South Braintree, Massachusetts, shoe company were shot and killed in a robbery. Police found the getaway car in a woods close by. A man seen in that car was traced to another car in a repair shop in West Bridgewater, Massachusetts. When the man came to get his car, police sped to the shop to arrest him. He escaped on a motorcycle before they got there. But two other men, Nicola Sacco and Bartolomeo Vanzetti, who went with him to the repair shop, were arrested.

Sacco and Vanzetti, Italian immigrants, were anarchists, members of an international movement who wanted to destroy all government in order to achieve justice for the poor. With the arrest of Sacco and Vanzetti, a local robbery case turned into an international political event. Many people believed they were arrested because they were poor immigrants and anarchists.

The prosecution's case was based on two facts: Sacco owned a pistol like the one used in the murders and both men were at the repair shop trying to claim an automobile seen in connection with the crime. Six .32-caliber bullets had been taken from the victims' bodies. Test shots fired from Sacco's pistol were compared to the six bullets. The markings on the test bullets matched only one of the bullets from the robbery. The prosecution said that one particular bullet came from Sacco's pistol; the defense said it did not. The jury believed the prosecution. Sacco and Vanzetti were convicted of murder and sentenced to death. Huge demonstrations protesting the verdict were held in Paris, Moscow, and cities in South America. Finally, in 1927, Massachusetts governor A. T. Fuller appointed a commission to advise him whether to grant clemency to Sacco and Vanzetti.

During the seven years the case made headlines, significant advances in ballistics had been made. Phillip Gravelle invented the comparison microscope, which allowed two bullets to be examined side by side; physicist John Fisher developed both a microscope that measured rifle grooves and angles with amazing accuracy and a helixometer, a lighted instrument that could be inserted into the barrel of a firearm so an examiner could see the rifling, or carvings, inside the barrel.[4]

At the 1927 hearing conducted by the governor's commission, the comparison microscope was used in a courtroom for the first time. Dr. Calvin Goddard, a ballistics expert, examined the bullets found at the robbery scene and declared the fatal bullet had been fired from Sacco's gun. A defense expert looked into the microscope and said, "Well, what do you know about that?"[5] The defense's remark seemed to agree with the firearms expert's opinion, and all chances for an appeal were lost. On August 23, 1927, Sacco and Vanzetti were executed.

THE SAINT VALENTINE'S DAY MASSACRE

These advances in ballistics also helped solve one of the most famous crimes in American history—the Saint Valentine's Day Massacre. On February 14, 1929, in Chicago, Illinois, two men disguised as policemen entered a garage and ordered seven members of bootlegger Bugs Moran's gang to put up their hands and face a wall. While the gang's backs were turned, two other men sneaked into the garage and machine-gunned them. Al Capone, probably America's most famous gangster, was believed to have ordered the massacre.

Over seventy cartridges from the crime scene were identified as having been fired from .45-caliber Thompson submachine guns. Ten months later, a policeman in St. Joseph, Michigan, was shot by a motorist he stopped for a traffic violation. The shooter's license plate number was traced to Fred Burke. Police discovered two .45-caliber Thompson submachine guns in his apartment. Using a comparison microscope, Dr. Goddard, who had testified in the Sacco and Vanzetti case, proved these were the weapons used in the Saint Valentine's Day Massacre. Burke was eventually captured and convicted of murder. He was sentenced to life in prison.[6]

The success of Goddard's laboratory convinced the first director of the FBI, J. Edgar Hoover, to make the bureau the center of scientific criminal investigative knowledge in the United States. In 1931, he instructed his agents to contact scientific experts for advice on training a staff to run a crime laboratory. On November 24, 1932, the FBI's Scientific Crime Detection Laboratory, as it was originally named, opened in a lounge in the Old Southern Railway Building in Washington, D.C. The site was chosen because the room contained a sink. In its first week, the lab worked on twenty cases. Today it analyzes thousands of cases each week.

Crude crime-solving tools in the original lab included a borrowed microscope, an ultraviolet light, and a drawing board. To X-ray a suspicious package for explosives, the lab had to use an X-ray machine from another government bureau. Eventually, a comparison microscope, test tubes, and a one-way mirror were added. In 1938, when the polygraph machine was invented, agents began conducting lie detector tests. FBI chemist Dr.

William Magee described the primitive lab test on a substance suspected of being dynamite: "They would take an extract, put it on an anvil, and hit it with a hammer. If it went poof, it was dynamite."[7]

In 1935, Hoover founded the National Police Academy to train law enforcement personnel how to use the FBI lab to solve crimes. In 1943, the name of the lab was changed to the FBI Laboratory. And in September 1975, the lab moved to its present site in the J. Edgar Hoover Building at Ninth Street and Pennsylvania Avenue, NW.

Forensic science has come a long way since J. Edgar Hoover established the FBI Scientific Crime Detection Laboratory in 1932. For example, today the FBI has over 200,000,000 fingerprints on file, handles almost 20,000 cases a year, and performs almost a million examinations on over 200,000 pieces of evidence. And today there are about 400 crime laboratories in the United States, and nearly 40,000 forensic scientists working in these laboratories.[8]

The FBI crime lab has become the most important law enforcement facility in America. Part of the lab's claim to fame is that it provides investigative services for all federal, state, and local law enforcement agencies absolutely free of charge. FBI examiners also testify to their results in court free of charge. There are only two requirements. First, law enforcement agencies must accept the FBI's results as final. Second, they agree the results will be made available to the suspect, even if the results show the suspect is innocent. In fact, in some of the FBI's forensic units, approximately one-third of the examinations result in a negative conclusion, meaning the suspect cannot be linked to the evidence.

Modern forensics investigation is a team effort, employing a wide range of professionals. Dentists study bite marks to help confirm the identity of a killer; toxicologists analyze poisons found in victims' blood, organs, and tissues; pathologists examine burn marks, knife wounds, and entry patterns in gunshot wounds; psychiatrists study evidence in serial crimes to come up with a psychological profile of the killer; anthropologists examine long-buried bones to determine their identity; and serologists perform tests on blood found on the victim and the suspect to see if they match.[9]

Not only have various professionals come into the spotlight of forensics, but scientific tools have moved into the forensic laboratory as well. For instance, special microscopes called scanning electron microscopes (SEMs) can magnify particles found at crime scenes by as much as two hundred thousand times. Other instruments can separate and identify chemicals found in complex mixtures. This identification allows forensic scientists to discover the original source of fibers, glass fragments, paint chips, and other physical evidence collected by crime investigators. Advanced forensic methods such as DNA analysis allow forensic scientists to examine bloodstains and discover who they came from.

In addition, portable lasers reveal fingerprints that would otherwise be impossible to see. Once discovered, modern chemicals can be put on these faint fingerprints to lift them off one surface and transfer them to another so that they can be brought into crime labs and analyzed. Advanced computer technology has made analysis and data collecting faster, and allowed vast amounts of information about criminals to be stored on tiny computer microchips. This information can be accessed instantly by police departments around the world.

The success of the FBI's crime laboratory opened police detectives' eyes to the value of science as an investigative tool, and thrust forensics to the forefront of crime solving. In fact, forensic analyses of crime scene evidence has become so important to successfully solving crimes that some experts predict that in the future, forensic experts will not be just scientists. Every police officer, too, will be a "science cop." And everyone involved in criminal investigations will be after the "threads of evidence" that will link the criminal to the crime.

1

HOW SCIENCE SOLVES CRIMES

On December 16, 1989, in Mountain Brook, Alabama, federal court judge Robert Vance received a small box in his mail. When he opened it, the box exploded, killing him and wounding his wife. Two days later, attorney Robert Robinson of Savannah, Georgia, was killed when he opened a package in his office and it exploded. That same day, a bomb was discovered among packages mailed to judges in the Atlanta federal courthouse.

And still another package bomb, delivered to a female employee of the National Association for the Advancement of Colored People (NAACP) legal counsel in Jacksonville, Florida, lay unopened while she ran errands. She did not return to the office that day, because her car broke down and she went home. That night, she heard about the explosion in Savannah. Fearing the package sent to her might also be a bomb, she called the Jacksonville bomb squad. The woman's car trouble saved her life.[1]

The FBI crime lab began what would become a year-long investigation of the bombings. Because Judge Vance was the first person murdered by these package bombs, the FBI named the case VANPAC. First, the Explosives Unit examined the remains of the bombs to analyze their components. The Jacksonville and Atlanta bombs, disarmed before they exploded, provided valuable information. It was believed the same person made all the bombs, as each bomb was made the same way—a steel pipe was filled with smokeless powder and placed inside a box. The powder would explode when a current from two C batteries ran through a lightbulb filament to a detonator. A thin piece of cardboard was inserted between two sheets of aluminum foil and placed between the batteries and the detonator. A string was tied to the box lid in such a way that when anyone opened the box, the string pulled out the cardboard, and the two sheets of aluminum foil touched, connecting the batteries and the detonator, making the bombs explode. In addition, investigators found that the insides of the boxes were painted with black enamel. And threatening letters were found inside the bombs that had been disarmed before they exploded.[2]

TEAMWORK IN ACTION

Pieces of the bomb fragments were sent to different units in the crime lab, each specializing in a particular area of crime detection. The DNA Analysis Unit worked on developing a DNA profile of the bomber from saliva found on the mailing labels and stamps. It was assumed that the bomber was the one who had licked them. The Hairs and Fibers Unit worked on finding where the string attached to the lid came from. Knot experts tried to match the knots in the string to a particular profession. The Materials Analysis Unit worked on identifying the black enamel paint. The Elemental Analysis Unit examined the nails used as shrapnel in the bombs, and identified the press in Taiwan on which the nails had been made. The Latent Fingerprint

Section found a partial print on the letter inside the Jacksonville bomb. The Chemistry/Toxicology Unit searched for the source of the smokeless powder. The Document Section searched for the typewriter on which the threatening letters had been typed and the manufacturer of the cardboard boxes.[3]

The Document Section scored first. The typewriter used to write the letters had a broken key that had been replaced with one that did not match the rest. Because the killer had sent his bombs to people involved in the legal profession, FBI agents searched the judicial files of each of the three states where bombs had been delivered. They tried to find documents written on a typewriter with one particular mismatched key. Among tens of thousands of pages of documents, a threatening letter that had been typed on the same machine was found in the Atlanta courthouse. The letter was found to have been written several years earlier by a man in Enterprise, Alabama. Officers searched his house, but found no evidence to link him to the bombings.

The explosive was analyzed and identified as Hercules Red Dot smokeless powder. Agents questioned store owners throughout the South to find anyone who sold a large quantity of Red Dot around the time the bombs were mailed. An agent of the Bureau of Alcohol, Tobacco, and Firearms (ATF) suggested investigators question a man named Walter Leroy Moody from Georgia, who had built a similar bomb in 1972. Moody had been convicted of possession of a bomb and served time in prison. His hatred of the judicial system was considered a possible motive for the bombs being mailed to judges and other members of the justice system.

Agents searched Moody's house, but no evidence was found connecting Moody to the bombs. However, agents did find a photograph of Moody's 1972 bomb, which was identical to the unknown bomber's 1989 bombs. Moody's wife said she bought supplies for him, and finally admitted she drove to Covington, Kentucky, to make copies of his threatening letter. The Latent

Fingerprint Section identified the partial print found on one of the letters as that of a part-time employee of a copy shop. He had left his print on the paper while loading the copy machine. That print was the clincher. It proved Mrs. Moody was telling the truth about copying the threatening letter. Walter Moody was convicted and sentenced to seven life terms plus four hundred years in prison. His capture and conviction were mainly due to the amazing techniques of forensic science.[4]

WHAT IS FORENSICS?

The word *forensics* means suitable for presentation in a court of law. Thus the goal of forensic investigation is to uncover enough accurate, convincing evidence from the crime scene to present in court during a trial. Without sufficient evidence, the district attorney has no case with which to prosecute a suspect.

Forensic investigation is the use of science to examine evidence and solve crimes. Just as members of a football team perform different functions in a game to score a touchdown, members of the forensic team perform different scientific jobs in criminal investigations to solve crimes. As you can see from the Moody bombing case, the "players" on the forensic team include someone from just about every scientific area, from chemists to biologists to medical technologists.

THE EVIDENCE

Evidence of a crime may be found anywhere, from the actual crime scene to a remote location miles away. And the evidence may be biological, such as fingerprints, blood, or even the corpse itself; or nonbiological, such as bullet cartridge casings, clothing fibers, or the pieces of a bomb. But all this evidence eventually ends up at the same place—the forensic laboratory, or crime lab. There, scientists trace where this evidence came from and may compare it with similar evidence found on the suspect. Then they use the results of their investigations to reconstruct a step-by-step account of how the crime was committed. All of their findings are then testified to in court.

THE FORENSIC TEAM

Determining the perpetrator of a crime is a team effort between criminal investigators and forensic scientists. All the different professional experts are vital in finding and analyzing the evidence, and in revealing the whole story of the crime—who committed the crime, how it was committed, when, where, and even why the crime was committed.

THE PATHOLOGIST

After the police, the medical examiner (ME) is the first forensic specialist involved in investigating a crime. The 1915 New York City law replacing the coroner with a medical examiner also authorized the examiner to decide on the need for an autopsy and to investigate all deaths resulting from violence, accident, suicide, or suspicious manner. The ME is a pathologist, a scientist who studies the nature and course of illness and disease by analyzing body tissues and fluids for bacteria, viruses, and poisons.

THE TOXICOLOGIST

A scientist who specializes in finding and examining drugs and poisonous substances in body fluid and tissue is called a toxicologist. A poison may be any substance that produces disease conditions, tissue injury, or in any way interrupts natural life processes when absorbed into the body. Most poisons, if taken in large enough doses, are lethal, meaning they result in death. Because all toxicologists are chemists as well, most forensic laboratories group the two specialties together. Thus the unit specializing in analyzing both poisonous and nonpoisonous chemicals is called the Chemistry/Toxicology Unit, or the Chem/Tox for short.

THE PHARMACOLOGIST

A partner of the toxicologist is the pharmacologist, who studies the effects of drugs or chemicals on the body. In particular, the pharmacologist studies how chemicals are absorbed by the body, where in the body they act, how they affect the body, and how chemicals are metabolized and excreted. The complete process a chemical goes through in the body is called metabolism.

THE SEROLOGIST

Serologists are scientists who study body fluids in humans and animals. In the early days of forensics, the science of serology was limited to determining whether a blood sample came from a human being or an animal. If from a human, serologists classified the blood into one of the four known blood groups (A, B, AB, or O). Each classification could apply to a huge number of people. Thus merely classifying the blood group found at a crime scene added little weight in proving a suspect was guilty.

In the 1970s, however, serologists discovered elements in blood and other body secretions that made it possible to match a sample found at a crime scene to a much smaller number of people. When the procedure to extract DNA from human cells and link it to a specific person was developed, serology became the star specialty on the forensic football team. And serologists rose from the position of water boy to quarterback.

DNA analysis not only helps prove a suspect guilty of a crime, it may also help prove the suspect innocent. For example, in April 1989, when a young woman was jogging through New York City's Central Park, a gang of men raped her, smashed her in the head with a rock, and left her to die. The police arrested twelve suspects and compared blood and semen samples from the men with samples taken from the victim. The results showed the samples did not come from any of the twelve suspects. Thus the men could not be convicted of the crime based on this particular evidence.[5]

THE PSYCHOLOGIST/PSYCHIATRIST

In the same way a police sketch artist takes information from a witness or victim of a crime and draws a physical picture of a criminal, a forensic psychiatrist or psychologist takes information about a case and then compiles a description of the type of person the police should be looking for. This psychological profile, or offender profile, as it is also called, includes a prediction of the perpetrator's race, religion, ethnic background, education, family, clothes preference, and motivation for committing the crime or crimes in question. Forensic psychiatrists are most often called on by the police to help catch serial killers.

THE TECHNOLOGIST

In today's increasingly technological world, gathering and analyzing crime scene evidence often depends on high-tech instruments. These instruments include computers that print out digital photographs of killers. But machinery is useless without someone to operate it. This is where the forensic technologist is sent into the game. From the medical lab technician, to the electrical engineer, to the computer whiz, these technologists are invaluable players on the forensic team.

THE POLYGRAPH TEST   One of the most well-known forensic tools is the polygraph exam, also called the lie detector test. Most people believe polygraphs can tell if a person is guilty or innocent, and that results from polygraphs are not admissible in court. Neither one of these beliefs is true.

The polygraph is an investigative tool used to help confirm information given to police by suspects. The exam does not test for the actual truth, but rather for what the subject believes to be true. Anybody who believes he is telling the truth is going to pass the test. And the results of polygraphs are allowed as evidence in a trial if both the prosecution and defense agree to admitting those results. In addition, a confession made during the test can be used in a trial as long as the polygraph test itself is not talked about in court.

The value of lie detector tests is based on the principle that people worry about being caught when they lie, and that fear causes physiological reactions that can be measured. The first lie-detecting machine, called the hydrophygmograph, was invented in 1895 and measured changes in pulse rate and blood pressure of the subject. In 1921, John Larsen developed an instrument that continuously recorded changes in blood pressure, pulse rate, and respiration during questioning. He named his machine the polygraph.[6]

At first, the polygraph was believed to be 100 percent accurate. The test became world famous in the 1930s, when Bruno Hauptmann, the accused kidnapper and killer of aviator Charles Lindbergh's baby, failed a lie detector exam. But in 1938, investigations in a kidnapping-murder case in Florida showed that a man who tested innocent was guilty, and that the person who later confessed was innocent. FBI director J. Edgar Hoover ordered agents to get rid of their polygraph machines.

When former president Richard Nixon asked the FBI to find out who was leaking secret information from the State Department in 1971, embarrassed FBI staff members had to borrow a lie detector machine from the New York City Police Department. That incident brought back the use of lie detector tests in criminal investigations.[7]

No one can be made to take a lie detector test. But if a suspect refuses to take the exam, that refusal casts doubt on the suspect's claim of innocence. On the other hand, if the suspect asks to take the test, investigators are more inclined to believe the suspect's claims. For example, before the 1994 Winter Olympics, when figure skater Tonya Harding's husband, Jeff Gillooly, was charged with masterminding the attack on Harding's competitor, Nancy Kerrigan, he wanted to make a deal with prosecutors for a lighter sentence by proving Harding knew about, and approved, the attack. Prosecutors made

Gillooly take a lie detector test to prove he was telling the truth about Harding before they would make the deal. When Gillooly passed the test, investigators started questioning Harding, who finally confessed her part in the scheme to keep Nancy Kerrigan out of the Olympics.[8]

One of the most famous polygraph exams was given to Jack Ruby, the man who killed Lee Harvey Oswald, accused assassin of President John F. Kennedy. According to conspiracy theories, Ruby knew Oswald and killed him to keep him from telling the truth about the assassination. Ruby demanded to take a polygraph exam to prove he was not part of a conspiracy. The test took place in Dallas, Texas, on July 18, 1964. Ruby was asked questions to cover all the conspiracy theories, such as, "Did you know Oswald?" "Were you involved in a conspiracy to kill the president?" "Were you linked to an organized crime element and paid off to silence Oswald?" Ruby passed the test. Although many people still believe Kennedy was killed as part of a conspiracy, the lie detector test proved Jack Ruby was not part of it.[9]

THE ANTHROPOLOGIST

Anthropology is the study of the biological and social characteristics of human beings. When a long-buried body is found, or exhumed from a grave, a forensic anthropologist examines the body for clues to who the person was and how the person died. For example, in 1991, when historians wanted to know for sure whether former United States President Zachary Taylor died in 1850 from gastroenteritis, swelling of the intestines, or arsenic poisoning, his body was exhumed for forensic examination. Chemical analysis of his remains showed the former president died of gastroenteritis.[10]

––––––––––––––

Every forensic investigation begins at the crime scene. Any evidence found there may prove to be the single clue needed to solve a case. The evidence might be trace (so small that only traces of it can be found), such as a speck of paint, the lead scraping a bullet has left on a bone, or human cells from a drop of blood smaller than the period at the end of this sentence. Or the evidence might be as large as a skull, the wall of a building, or the entire contents of a serial killer's apartment.

In December 1988, Pan Am Flight 103 exploded over Lockerbie, Scotland, killing 270 people. Out of millions of pieces of wreckage, it was one piece of plastic the size of a thumbnail that identified the bombers. Atlanta child killer Wayne Williams was caught when a few hairs and fibers were found in his home. A partial fingerprint on a forty-year-old postcard proved a Detroit archbishop was an agent for the Nazis during World War II. And several minute specks of green particles identified the woman who killed two people by putting cyanide in Excedrin capsules.[11]

Forensic investigators take pieces of evidence, like pieces of a jigsaw puzzle, and shift them into different positions until each piece fits perfectly into the finished puzzle. And just like fitting all the pieces of a jigsaw puzzle together, when all the evidence relating to a crime is fitted together, the pieces form one big picture. The big picture in forensic investigation is the answer to the question, "Who done it?"

2

BIOLOGICAL EVIDENCE

In 1974, newlyweds Patricia and Claude Giesick went to New Orleans, Louisiana, on their honeymoon. While standing on a street corner waiting for the light to change, Patricia was pushed into the street and killed by a hit-and-run driver.

Because Claude had insured his new wife for $350,000 in a double indemnity life insurance policy, investigators were suspicious. They discovered Claude had rented two cars the day before the accident. The second car was traced to the rental agency and searched. Two strands of hair were found stuck to the tie rod underneath the car. When examined under a microscope, the hairs were consistent with Patricia Giesick's hair. Her husband had rented the car that killed her. Confronted with this indisputable biological evidence, Claude confessed that he had hired a hit-and-run driver to run over his wife when he pushed her off the curb. Claude killed her to collect the insurance money.[1]

Tiny "threads of evidence," like the two strands of hair that trapped Patricia Giesick's murderer, have been the clues that have caught countless criminals. Human, or biological, evidence can be a strand of hair, a piece of skin, a severed body part, body fluids such as blood, saliva, urine, and semen, or any other evidence found at the crime scene that came from a living person.

BLOOD

In crime detection, serology means the identification of bloodstains. Serologists use tests to determine whether a bloodstain came from a human or an animal, and the bloodstain's type. Tests can also determine the animal from which the blood came.

WHAT BLOOD TYPE ARE YOU?

If the blood found at the crime scene is human, serologists determine the blood type. Human red blood cells may contain one, or both, or neither of two antigens, named A or B. Your blood, therefore, is one of four types: A, B, AB, or O (meaning you have neither the A nor the B antigen).

A calculation has been done on the percentages of people in the United States who have each of the four blood types. Type AB is the most rare. Therefore, finding type AB blood at a crime scene is very useful in reducing the list of suspects. In contrast, type O blood is the most common type, and finding type O blood at a crime scene would only reduce the list of suspects by half. Thus a blood type match between the suspect and the victim only means the suspect *could* have committed the crime.[2] A blood type match does not mean the suspect *did* commit the crime.

GENETIC MARKERS

Forensic serologists also look for genetic markers in blood to narrow down a list of suspects. These markers function the same way in all humans, but they do not have the same chemical structure. For example, one type of genetic marker is an enzyme in the blood. Ten different types of the enzyme phosphogluco-mutase (PGM) have been identified. So while two people may have the same blood type, there is less chance they will have the same blood type *and* all the same PGM types. Finding just three or four genetic markers in a blood sample is enough evidence to prove that blood came from one person in a million.[3]

A case in Maynardville, Tennessee, illustrates the use of genetic markers to catch a murderer. When a young woman was abducted and beaten to death, her husband's friend was suspected of the murder. But police had no physical evidence to prove he committed the crime. Hairs and fibers found in the woman's house, that matched the friend's, could have been left there anytime, because the friend visited the couple often. Police sent the FBI's serology lab the new Levi's jeans the man had worn on the day of the murder. A small bloodstain was found in one of the pockets.

When confronted with the bloodstain, the suspect said he had bloodied his knuckles in a fistfight. Tests were run for all twelve known genetic markers. Three of the enzymes could not possibly have come from the suspect, but were consistent with the victim's blood. The assumption was he skinned his knuckles when he punched the woman, then put his hands in his pockets. Genetic markers were the evidence that led to the suspect's conviction.[4]

The disadvantage of genetic markers is that once blood is outside the body, the enzymes deteriorate. By the time the bloodstain is dry, several of the markers have disappeared. And since most blood samples submitted for tests are dry, it is impossible to identify many of the genetic markers contained in that blood, because they have already deteriorated.

BLOOD SPATTERING

Forensic serologists must also have an understanding of physics when examining blood found at crime scenes. Not only do the chemicals found in blood link criminals to crimes, but patterns made by blood tell an important story as well. These blood patterns are called blood spatter. Blood is a liquid and, like any fluid, will act according to the laws of physics. By observing the bloodstain's size, shape, distribution, location, angle of impact, and the surface it was found on, information can be learned about what took place at the crime scene.

If blood spatter is found on someone, it indicates he or she was at the scene when a bloody object or person was hit. (People can contact blood when rendering aid to a victim. The pattern of the spatter will make that clear.) The harder someone is hit, the smaller the blood spatter. So when someone is stabbed, which requires a lot of force, the blood spatter will be smaller; a punch in the nose, on the other hand, which takes less force to deliver and causes blood to drip straight down to the floor, will leave larger blood spots.

Blood spattering can tell something about the victim, too. If a series of elongated drops of blood several feet apart is found, this means the victim was probably running. Round drops of blood closer together means the victim was probably walking. A large stain on a surface, clothing for example, is called a contact stain, and means that surface was in touch with a bloody object, such as a knife. A large bloodstain with an area containing no blood means something blocked the spatter of blood. In this case, finding the person or object that blocked the spray of blood will be an important clue because the blood will be on that person or object.[5]

CAST-OFF STAINS   Straight lines of elongated bloodstains are called cast-off stains. These bloodstains are caused when blood is thrown from a moving object, such as a knife, as it changes direction. A typical example is when a killer stabs his victim repeatedly with a knife. Each time the killer draws back his knife, he throws off another line of blood. Cast-off stains at a crime scene can tell how many times the victim was hit. The total number of blows is always one more than the number of stains, because the first time the victim is hit, the weapon has no blood on it.[6]

BLOOD SPATTER UNCOVERS A KILLER   Blood spatter was the main evidence that convicted former Green Beret Dr. Jeffrey MacDonald of killing his wife, Colette, and his two daughters, Kristen and Kimberly, in their home at Fort Bragg Army Base in North Carolina in February 1970. They had been stabbed repeatedly, and his daughters had also been battered with a blunt instrument. Dr. MacDonald claimed hippies spaced-out on drugs committed the murders. He said he had been stabbed, knocked unconscious, and left for dead in the entry hall. When he came to, he found his family murdered. But the blood spatter said otherwise.

Paul Stombaugh, then chief of the FBI's Chemistry/Toxicology Unit, found that each member of the MacDonald family had a different blood type. He identified the blood types found in each room and on the murder weapons to show where in the house each person was stabbed or hit and with what weapon. Then, using blood spatter evidence, he filled in the blow-by-blow account of the murders.

The top sheet on the bed in Kristen's room had a large bloodstain. Yet there was no bloodstain on the bottom sheet. The bloodstain on the top sheet was type A, Mrs. MacDonald's type. The rest of the blood in Kristen's room was type O, Kristen's type. Stombaugh theorized that if the sheet had been placed on the floor of Kristen's room, and Mrs. MacDonald's body were held over it before being placed on it, she would have bled directly onto the sheet. Then her body could have been covered with the sheet and put back on the bed.

The bedspread in Kimberly's room had type AB blood on it, Kimberly's blood type, and the same type found on the club used to murder her. This stain was from a transfer of blood. An object having type AB blood on it, most likely the club, was placed on the bedspread. Stombaugh theorized that Dr. Mac-Donald hit Kimberly with the club while she was in another room, then carried her into her bedroom and, as indicated by the AB blood spatters on the wall, hit her again with the club.

None of Jeffrey MacDonald's blood, which was Type B, was found in the entry hall. Based on the blood spatter evidence, the jury believed MacDonald was lying and found him guilty. He was sentenced to three consecutive life sentences, the most severe penalty he could receive.[7]

Blood spatter is also useful in determining whether a death was a suicide or a homicide. When the body of a man was found hanging in his Texas home, the walls and ceiling of the room were sprinkled with tiny drops of blood. It appeared he had been beaten, then hanged. But a closer look at the blood spatter revealed a different story.

The man's body had not been discovered for nearly four days. During that time, flies had fed on the corpse, then landed on the walls with blood on their legs. What cinched the case was the fact that a lightbulb that had been left on in the room had no blood on it, because it was too hot for the flies to land on. If the man had been beaten, there would have been blood spatter on the lightbulb. Blood really does tell all.[8] This case was a suicide.

FORENSIC DENTISTRY

Another important player on the forensic team is the forensic dentist. When a body is burned or otherwise brutalized beyond recognition, sometimes the teeth are the only identifying parts of the body that remain. Because everyone's teeth are different, having distinct characteristics such as shape, bite pattern, chemical makeup, and coloration, forensic dentists can compare the teeth found in the remains of a victim with dental X rays of people who detectives think might be the victim. Forensic dentists look for matches between the victim's teeth and the dental X rays of possible victims, such as evidence of fillings, root canals, and damage caused by gum disease. If one of the dental X rays matches the dental remains of the victim, detectives will know who the victim was.

TEETH MARKS

Sometimes criminals, for whatever reason, bite their victims, leaving teeth marks. In cases where bite marks are not readily visible, ultraviolet light shined on a victim's skin can illuminate the marks. Melanocytes, skin cells that produce the dark pigment responsible for tanning, form around the margins of wounds. These melanocytes absorb ultraviolet light. When illuminated, the bite marks appear, and may be photographed with a scale, such as a ruler, beside them to indicate the exact size of the bite marks. A forensic dentist can compare these bite marks with those made by a suspect to see if they match.[9]

THE WOOD CHIPPER MURDER CASE

In a case known as the "wood chipper murder," Richard Crafts of Newtown, Connecticut, was accused of killing his wife, Helle, on November 18, 1986, then cutting her body into parts that he placed in plastic bags, and then shredded in a wood chipper. Crafts claimed his wife, a flight attendant, had gone to visit her mother after working on a flight to Europe. The police talked to Mrs. Crafts's mother, who was not expecting Helle to visit at all. Crafts told police he had rented the wood chipper to get rid of some limbs that had fallen during a snowstorm. But a highway worker driving a snowplow claimed to have seen Crafts using the wood chipper near Lake Zoar, not far from his home, at 4:00 A.M. during the snowstorm.

Police sifted through the debris found at the lake where the highway worker had seen Crafts, and found pieces of bone, fingernail, toenail, two teeth, dental crowns, fingers, hairs, and plastic. Hairs discovered at the lake were found to match hairs taken from Helle Crafts's hairbrush. Police also found a chainsaw in the river, which was traced to Richard Crafts, and on which were found human tissues and blond hairs. In addition, marks made by a wood-chipping machine found on wood chips near the lake matched those found on chips in a woodlot near Crafts's home and in the back of his truck.

Crafts claimed not to know where the human remains found at the lake came from. But Dr. C. P. Karazulas testified that after comparing the teeth to Helle Crafts's dental X rays, he could positively say a tooth and a gold crown came from Helle Crafts. His tests were confirmed by a forensic dentist, Dr. Lowell Levine. The teeth told the tale, and Richard Crafts was convicted of murdering his wife.[10]

FINGERPRINTS

A little before midnight, on October 1, 1993, twelve-year-old Polly Klaas and two girlfriends were having a slumber party in Polly's Petaluma, California, home. Suddenly a man dressed in dark clothing and carrying a knife walked into Polly's bedroom and ordered the girls to lie down on the floor. He tied their hands and pulled pillowcases over their heads. Then he kidnapped Polly.

As is usual in cases of kidnapping, the FBI was called in and began searching Polly's bedroom for fingerprints. Agents sprinkled red fluorescent powder on the surfaces of her room, then turned off the regular lights, put on tinted goggles, and turned on an alternate light source (ALS). Viewed through filtered goggles, the ALS illuminates fingerprints, shoe prints, and bloodstains that cannot be seen with the naked eye under normal lighting conditions. Of the many fingerprints found in Polly Klaas's room, there was only one that could not be accounted for. That was a partial palm print on the upper rail of Polly's bunk bed.

Two months later, some torn children's clothes were found on a hillside in Petaluma. Police decided to run a computer search of traffic incidents on the night Polly was kidnapped to see if anyone was stopped near that location. The search showed that an hour and a half after she was abducted, two sheriff's deputies reported a man named Richard Allen Davis had gotten his car stuck in a ditch near the site. Because the deputies had not stopped Davis for a traffic violation and were unaware of Polly's kidnapping just ninety minutes before, they had no reason to call in Davis's drivers' license to check if he had a criminal record. They merely helped him get his car out of the ditch and sent him on his way.

Now the police checked. Records showed that Richard Allen Davis had spent seventeen of the last twenty-one years in prison for burglary, assault, and kidnapping, and was even at that moment on parole. He was arrested on suspicion of kidnapping. Davis confessed, saying he was high on beer and marijuana laced with PCP that night and had no idea why he kidnapped Polly. He said he strangled her after realizing he would be sent back to prison if she identified him. Then he added a tragic postscript: Polly was still alive nearby in the woods when the deputies helped him get his car out of the ditch. He returned to the site later and strangled her. Davis led police to Polly's body on December 4, two months after she was kidnapped.[11]

The FBI lab examined a hair sample from Davis and found it to be consistent with the single unidentified hair found in Polly's bedroom. Davis's palm print matched the partial one found on Polly's bed. The palm print match was the crucial evidence that identified Davis as the killer. If he had killed Polly

Klaas only a few years earlier, the technology used to find it would not have been in use, and that print would not have been found. On June 18, 1996, Richard Allen Davis was found guilty of all ten charges against him, including kidnapping and murdering Polly Klaas.[12] On August 5, 1996, he was sentenced to death by lethal injection.

THE EVOLUTION OF FINGERPRINTS

Early civilizations identified criminals by branding them with tattoos or cutting off their fingers or hands. In the early 1800s, policemen with supposedly photographic memories would visit prisons to look at convicts and memorize their faces for the future. In 1879, Frenchman Alphonse Bertillon invented his body measurement method to identify people. Fingerprints were used for official purposes in the United States for the first time in 1882, when an officer of the United States Geological Survey who was mapping North America used his own print to prevent forgery of his supply orders.

Then, in 1903, a criminal named Will West was sentenced to Leavenworth Prison, in Fort Leavenworth, Kansas. When West's Bertillon measurements were taken, a clerk found that another prisoner, also named Will West, had the same measurements. Although not related, the two men looked strikingly alike. The only physical trait that was different about them was their fingerprints. The very next day, Leavenworth Prison dropped the Bertillon method and started using fingerprints to identify inmates.[13]

In 1924, Congress established the FBI's Identification Division as the national repository of all fingerprint records. For the first time, a criminal arrested for one crime could be connected to another crime committed in a different place at a different time—all by means of looking at the ridges on his fingertips. Today the Identification Division is the largest unit within the FBI, employing more than 2,600 people. The Identification Division contains more than 200,000,000 prints repre-

senting more than 68,000,000 people on file in t.
Criminal Justice Information Services Division.[14]

WHAT ARE FINGERPRINTS?

Everyone is born with a unique set of tiny ridges in the skin covering the last part of each finger on the side opposite the fingernail. These ridges are your fingerprints. They will never change, no matter how long you live. You can see these ridges if you look at your fingers in strong light. You will see the ridges are not continuous. They stop, start, divide, and make patterns—loop, whorls, or arches. It is the arrangement and relationship of these patterns that make your fingerprints unique, and thus identifiable. Even if the tips of your fingers are burned, the ridges will grow back in the same pattern you were born with.

Along the ridges of your fingertips are thousands of sweat pores. Sweat carries the body oils naturally found on fingers. So whenever you touch something, your perspiration is transferred from your fingertips to that object, leaving an outline of your fingers' ridge patterns on whatever your fingers touch. Even clean hands have enough body oil to leave faint fingerprints. Because no two fingerprints are alike, this impression can be used to prove that a particular person was in a specific place or handled a specific object.[15]

IDENTIFYING FINGERPRINTS

Knowing where to look for fingerprints and how to develop them can mean the difference between cracking a case or filing it under "Unsolved Mysteries." In one case, bank robbers carefully wiped down the apartment they had lived in while planning a robbery, even putting all the dirty dishes into the dishwasher. But when they left, they forgot to turn on the machine. All the fingerprints in the apartment had been wiped away, but police found the robbers' fingerprints on all the dirty dishes.

If a fingerprint is visible to the naked eye, it is called a patent print. A print invisible to the naked eye is called a latent print. Latent prints can be made visible by many methods, depending on what material the print is found on.

IODINE FUMING In the late 1800s, it was discovered that iodine fumes react with body fats and oils to make fingerprints composed of those substances visible. In the iodine fuming method of lifting fingerprints, crystals of iodine are placed in a glass beaker and heated in a fume hood, producing a violet vapor. When the object containing the fingerprints is held over the vapor, the vapors condense back to crystals along the pattern of lines created by any fingerprints on the object. Iodine fuming is especially useful in lifting prints from rubber gloves.

Whatever method is used to identify fingerprints, a permanent copy of the print has to be made. This is called lifting, because in the 1920s prints were actually lifted off the material they were on by using the sticky side of rubber patches made for automobile inner tubes. Today the preferred method is to photograph the print. By placing various filters over the camera lens, it is even possible to photograph prints that are invisible in ordinary light.

SILVER NITRATE AND NINHYDRIN In the 1950s, scientists found that ninhydrin, the chemical most commonly used in fingerprint developing today, reacts with amino acids or protein matter usually found in perspiration to make them visible. And silver nitrate combines with invisible body salts to form the visible chemical compound sodium chloride. These substances, used in this order (otherwise the prints will be destroyed), find fingerprints left on wood or other porous surfaces.

Ninhydrin is especially good for developing prints on paper. In an Ohio murder case, the victim's body was found in his car, which had been pushed into the Ohio River. The only item found in the car that the victim's family could not identify was a map of the local area. The map was put in a toaster oven and slowly dried. Then it was sprayed with ninhydrin and steamed. Several prints immediately materialized. The prints were linked to a suspect, who apparently needed the map to find the river.

SUPERGLUE   In the 1970s, the discovery of new chemicals led to new techniques in making fingerprints visible. One method, first used by crime labs in 1982, employs a product used by millions of people every day—superglue. Its use to lift fingerprints was discovered by accident. A British policeman using the product to repair a cracked film-processing tank in a darkroom noticed the glue enhanced fingerprints left on the side of the tank. He tried it on other surfaces and found it produced distinct, raised prints.

In the superglue fuming method, the glue is heated in a beaker, and the object on which fingerprints have been made is held over the beaker. As the cyanoacrylate vapors in superglue condense, they stick to body oils left by the ridges of the fingers, making the pattern visible. Colored dyes are then used to make the prints stand out against the background. Superglue fuming is the method used to lift fingerprints off aluminum foil, rubber bands, Styrofoam, and other plastic products.

LASERS   Like Sherlock Holmes's magnifying glass, laser beams are used in the search for fingerprints. The laser method was also discovered by accident. In the mid-1970s, it seemed as if every time Canadian researchers turned on their lasers, their experiments were complicated by the presence of fingerprints. There is an old saying that "one man's headache is another man's pot of gold." Law enforcement officials took that saying to heart, realizing that while the fingerprints might be a problem to the researchers using lasers, to forensics experts, laser beams were a terrific new tool for visualizing fingerprints.

Lasers seem to work better on old evidence. In 1975, the United States Department of Justice initiated deportation proceedings against Valerian Trifa, a former archbishop of the

Romanian Orthodox Church of America. The Justice Department accused Trifa of concealing his membership in the fascist Iron Guard, Romania's pro-Nazi Party, during World War II. Trifa denied the charges, and it seemed impossible to find any hard evidence against him.

In 1982, however, the then West German government produced a postcard Trifa had sent to a high-ranking Nazi official in 1942. On the card, Trifa pledged his loyalty to the Nazi Party. The West Germans refused to allow the FBI to use any potentially destructive processes on what they considered a historic document. So, agents used a laser to examine the postcard. A left thumbprint was found, which was identical to the inked print Trifa had given when he became an American citizen. This was proof Trifa was a Nazi war criminal, and he was deported in 1984.[16]

DUSTING POWDER When President John F. Kennedy was assassinated in Dallas, Texas, on November 22, 1963, police found a rifle near a window in the Texas School Book Depository, where the shots came from. Cardboard book cartons had been placed around the window. The right palm print of Lee Harvey Oswald was found on the rifle's stock, but this was not proof of his guilt, as someone could have put the rifle there to put the blame on Oswald.

Detectives searched the area for latent prints. Oswald's fingerprints and palm prints were developed on three of the book cartons. But Oswald worked in the building, so it would be expected to find his prints there. What the police had to prove was that these were fresh prints, that Oswald had been at that window within a few hours of the time of the shooting. Since fingerprints cannot be dated, how could they prove the prints were fresh? Then Dallas detectives made a lucky mistake.

Cardboard is porous. So detectives should have used the silver nitrate method of developing fingerprints on the boxes. They had mistakenly used dusting powder and still found prints. Why? Fingerprint experts experimented with dusting powder and discovered the powder would show prints for up to three hours after they had been made. Then body fluids would be absorbed into the cardboard, preventing prints from showing. Oswald's prints had been developed with dusting powder, which proved he had been at the window within the previous three hours, during the time when the assassination took place.[17]

COMPUTERS AND FINGERPRINTS

Today, every time a suspect is arrested, he or she is fingerprinted. A copy of the fingerprints is sent to the identification system of the state the person is arrested in, and another goes to the Identification Division of the FBI's Criminal Justice Information Services Division in Washington, D.C. At the same time, police can access the FBI's and other identification systems via computer to learn if their suspect is wanted by another law enforcement agency, and if so, the status and last known address of the suspect.

Computers were used for the first time in fingerprint identification in 1968, after the assassination of Dr. Martin Luther King Jr. on the balcony of the Lorraine Hotel in Memphis, Tennessee. Detectives found a left thumbprint on the rifle from which the fatal bullet was believed to have been fired. Latent prints were found on a pair of binoculars. Police also had the alias the killer used when he checked into the hotel—Eric S. Galt. But they had no suspect to match with the prints or the alias. Police tracked "Eric Galt" to hotel rooms in several states and found many paper items with fingerprints on them. One good print, identical to the prints found on the rifle and binoculars, was lifted off a map found in a hotel in Atlanta, Georgia.

Using the latent print and a description of the assassin, a computerized search compared the latent print to all current fugitives known to the bureau—about 53,000 people at that time. The search narrowed down the possible matches to 1,900.

Agents pulled all 1,900 fingerprint cards, 100 suspects at a time. Amazingly, when agent Bobby Erwin got to the fifth card in his stack, he spotted the print from the man known as Eric Galt. "I saw this one, and I almost fell out of my chair," he said. "That's how we finally identified James Earl Ray as the man who killed Dr. King."[18] Ray's prints were in the file because he had escaped from a midwestern prison where he was serving time for robbery. He eventually pleaded guilty and was sentenced to ninety-nine years in prison.[19]

Prints that are not clear enough to be used for comparative purposes can be further developed in an image-enhancer computer, which converts the print into a digital image. For an examiner to decide that two prints have been made by the same person, every single characteristic of every identifiable ridge must be exactly the same.

ATTEMPTS TO ERASE FINGERPRINTS

For every way forensic experts find to develop a print, criminals try ways to erase them. They have tried sandpaper, dental sanders, and even acid, but ridges on fingers are several layers of skin deep and not easily destroyed. In the 1930s, John Dillinger, once named the FBI's Public Enemy Number 1, tried to destroy his prints by paying a surgeon $5,000 to cut off his fingerprints. The operation destroyed his fingerprints in the center of each finger above the first joint, but the ridges outside that small center section were left intact. That was enough to make a match when people doubted the man later shot and killed by the FBI outside Chicago's Biograph Theater was Dillinger.

In 1990, Miami police arrested a suspect in a drug case who had erased his fingerprints by slicing the skin on his fingertips into small pieces and transplanting those pieces onto other fingers. When his fingertips healed, he had new prints in which broken ridges ran in all directions. Thus it was impossible to link him to previous crimes by comparing his prints. But, Tommy Moorefield, an FBI latent print specialist, cut photographs of these scrambled prints into small pieces and began fitting the ridge patterns together. He restored small sections of several prints to their original pattern, like fitting together a jigsaw puzzle. Then specialists in the FBI's Technical Section matched them to those of a fugitive convicted in another major drug case. That comparison led to the suspect's conviction.

FINGERPRINTS TO IDENTIFY BODIES

When bodies are found burned or decomposed beyond recognition, besides using dental records, fingerprints are another way to identify the bodies if the skin on the fingers remains relatively intact. For example, the marines killed in the bombing of their Beirut, Lebanon, barracks in 1983; soldiers killed in Vietnam; and the astronauts and special passengers aboard the space shuttle Challenger in 1986, were all identified by their fingerprints.

To return shriveled or badly wrinkled skin on a corpse to a natural shape in order to obtain a fingerprint, forensic experts can soak it in water, heat it for a short time in a microwave, or inject it with a chemical substance called tissue builder. If the epidermis, the top layer of skin, has been damaged, it can be cut off, and usable prints can be obtained from the second layer of skin, the dermis. Sometimes the ridge detail on the outer part of the skin has been mutilated but is still visible on the inner side. Then the skin can be turned inside out and printed. In one incredible procedure, decomposing finger skin is sliced off, bathed in alcohol, and then slipped over the forensic scientist's own fingers and printed.

EYE PRINTS

Besides our fingers, other parts of our bodies have unique prints as well. The eyes are one example. Like the pattern of ridges on a person's fingers, blood vessels in the retinas of our eyes have a pattern not shared by any other person. Some police departments take photographs of arrested suspects' retinas in addition to taking their fingerprints. A scanner photographs the retinal patterns on the backs of the suspects' eyes, and the patterns are stored in the scanner system's computer memory. The computer can compare the retinal patterns of a suspect with other patterns stored in its memory to see if there is a match. The accurateness of scanners has encouraged businesses such as banks, nuclear weapons plants, and missile-launching sites to use retinal scanners to identify employees with clearance to enter maximum security areas.

When Patricia Giesick's husband hired the hit-and-run driver to kill her, the two strands of hair found underneath the rental car that hit her were consistent with her hair color and type. But they *could* have come from someone else who had that hair color and type. And when the unidentified hair found in Polly Klaas's bedroom was shown to be consistent with a hair sample from Richard Allen Davis, that consistency only meant the hair *could* have come from Davis. It could also have come from someone else who had that hair type. And when Colette MacDonald's blood type was found on the top sheet of the bed in her daughter Kristen's room, it was assumed the blood was Colette's. But it *could* have come from someone else who had that blood type.

So how do forensic scientists prove that out of all the people in the world, the hairs found stuck to the underside of a rental car came from the victim and no one else? That out of all the people in the world, the blood found on the top sheet of a child's bedroom belonged to her mother and no one else? That out of all the people in the world, the hair found in a kidnapped child's bedroom belonged to her kidnapper and no one else? Today, the answer is simple: they go after the genes.

3

ENTER DNA

FINGERPRINTS OF MODERN FORENSICS

The hottest forensic evidence at crime scenes today is a fingerprint that does not necessarily come from a person's hands. This evidence is the blueprint that makes every human being different from every other human being. It can be found in blood from a stab wound, saliva on the envelope of a ransom note, perspiration on a sweatband, or on hair from a person's head. This new fingerprint is called DNA.

WHAT IS DNA?

Why all the excitement over DNA? Short for deoxyribonucleic acid, DNA is the fundamental substance of all living things. It is found in the nucleus of all cells, except red blood cells, which have no nucleus. It is composed of a chain of four nucleotide base chemicals. The four nucleotide bases are adenine (A), guanine (G), cytosine (C), and thymine (T). There are an infinite number of ways the almost three billion of these four base chemicals in the DNA chain can be arranged. And it is how these nucleotide bases are arranged, or sequenced, that determines our genetic code—the characteristics that make each one of us unique.

DNA is found in the body's chromosomes, twenty-three pairs of coiled, threadlike molecules, which are located in each cell's nucleus (again, except red blood cells, which have no nucleus). The DNA in our chromosomes consists of small units called genes, arranged in a chain, along each chromosome. Our genes determine our hereditary characteristics, such as eye, skin, and hair color, height and build, intelligence, and even athletic ability.[1]

JUNK DNA

Most of the gene sequences in DNA are the same in all of us. However, what makes DNA analysis so valuable to forensic scientists is that each of us also has small sections of DNA between the genes that are not found in any other person. Called junk DNA, these sections consist of different triplet combinations of the four nucleotide bases, repeated over and over again, like the cars of a freight train. Identified by the code letters A, C, T, and G, an example of one of these triplets might be ACT, AGT, ACT, AGT, repeated again and again. Very few people have the same number of repeating sequences (also called tandem repeats) of these triplets. The only exception is identical twins. Identical twins come from the same sperm cell and egg cell, and therefore have identical chromosomes, thus identical DNA.

GENETIC FINGERPRINTS

Junk DNA is found in blood, saliva, perspiration, semen, vaginal fluid, skin tissue, bone marrow, dental pulp, and hair. By analyzing junk DNA, forensic experts can make a genetic "fingerprint," called a DNA profile, of the tandem repeats of the genetic code letters. If the tandem repeats analyzed from a sample of blood taken from the suspect match the tandem repeats found at the crime scene, that match, while not proof the suspect committed the crime, is proof the suspect was at the crime scene. So even if suspects wear gloves while committing crimes, if they leave any body cells at the scene, a unique DNA print can be made of those cells that will place them at the scene of the crime just as surely as if they had left a fingerprint from their own hands.[2]

For example, a DNA match was the basis of the prosecution's case against former professional football player O. J. Simpson in the June 12, 1994, murders of his ex-wife, Nicole Brown Simpson, and her friend, Ronald Goldman. A DNA match was made by comparing the tandem repeats in blood samples taken from the crime scene with tandem repeats taken from blood samples drawn from Simpson. The defense counterattacked the evidence by saying the police planted the drops of Simpson's blood found at the crime scene and in his car, a Ford Bronco. In spite of the DNA evidence, the jury found there was "reasonable doubt" whether Simpson committed the double murder, and acquitted him of all charges.

DNA in Forensic Investigations

DNA analysis was originally developed to study the inheritance of diseases, both to identify the disease-causing genes in families known to have inherited diseases, and to predict the chances of a family member getting the disease. The use of DNA for forensic purposes was pioneered in the early 1980s by British geneticist Dr. Alec Jeffreys of the University of Leicester. Britain's national forensic lab began comparing DNA in 1986. In the United States, the FBI officially began accepting requests for DNA comparisons in 1988. The results were so astounding that the FBI's Serology Unit changed its name to the DNA Analysis Unit. Today the FBI performs twenty-five hundred DNA tests a year for federal, state, and local prosecutors.[3]

There are two different scientific tests currently in use to make a DNA profile—RFLP tests, and PCR tests. Both are based on comparing DNA fragments found on specific sites on chromosomes. These sites are called polymorphic markers. DNA profiles analyze the lengths of at least three polymorphic marker sites.

RFLP TESTS

In RFLP testing, which stands for restriction fragment length polymorphisms, DNA is extracted from blood, hair, saliva, semen, or any other human tissue samples. Then special enzymes (proteins produced by living cells), called restriction enzymes, are injected into the DNA. Like finding a needle in a haystack, restriction enzymes find polymorphic marker sites embedded in long strands of DNA. Once found, the enzymes snip the polymorphic marker strands from the longer strands of DNA, resulting in many segments of DNA, each a different length. The process is like taking a long rope and randomly cutting it at different places, so you end up with several pieces of rope, each a different length. RFLP tests take several weeks to complete and require a lot of DNA in very good condition.

The snipped DNA segments are then placed in a gel. To separate the different polymorphic markers from one another, they are subjected to an electrical charge (called electrophoresis) that pulls them down the length of the gel. Next, the gel is transferred to a nylon membrane, which fixes the fragments in place. Then radioactive probes (DNA molecules that attach to specific DNA sites) "tag" the tandem repeat sequences, like pinning price tags to clothes in a store. Next, a piece of X-ray film is placed on the nylon membrane. The radioactive material in the probes produces a picture of differently shaped black bands on the X-ray film. Called an autoradiograph, or autorad for short, the black bands look similar to the bar codes on items in a supermarket.

Modern forensic techniques can isolate polymorphic markers from as few as twenty cells, a fraction of the number of cells contained in a single drop of blood. To determine whether two samples of DNA come from the same person, forensic scientists compare the pattern and lengths of the autorad bands made from cells taken from the suspect (usually by means of a blood sample drawn from the suspect) to the autorad bands made from cell evidence taken at the crime scene to see if they match.[4] Forensic scientists estimate the chance that a properly conducted RFLP test will incorrectly identify a person's tissue samples are less than one in a million.[5]

PCR TESTS

The second kind of forensic DNA test is called PCR-amplification testing. PCR stands for polymerase chain reaction. Unlike RFLP tests, a PCR analysis takes only a few days to complete and requires only small amounts of DNA. It does not matter if that DNA is contaminated, or degraded, by bacteria. In PCR testing, polymerase enzymes are used to amplify, or copy, the tandem repeat sequences of DNA. Think of PCR testing like a genetic Xerox machine, spewing out copy after copy of tandem repeats.

One PCR method involves comparing the DNA in one of several genes having code letter sequences that can vary only slightly from person to person. The chance of this test incorrectly matching a crime scene sample is only about one in several thousand.[6] A newer PCR testing procedure developed by Dr. Thomas Caskey of the Baylor College of Medicine in Houston, Texas, is even more accurate. Caskey's technique involves comparing short triplet repeat sequences in as many as thirteen locations on a sample of DNA—sites in which the number of repeats varies widely from person to person. In this test, the odds that the match could have occurred by chance are about one in one hundred thousand.[7]

DNA Evidence in Sexual Assaults

Before DNA testing, rape cases were the most difficult to solve. Only half of all reported rapes ended in arrests and, of those, less than half the suspects were convicted. These figures were the lowest conviction rate for any violent crime. But now, DNA analysis of semen collected from vaginal swabs of the victim can be compared with DNA analysis of semen from the suspect.

In November 1991, a Ritchie, Illinois, man was murdered and his wife raped and shot in the head at point-blank range. A year and a half later, police still had no leads. Then, in 1993, a forensic technologist entered the DNA profile developed from the killer's semen into Illinois's newly operational DNA data bank. The computer identified the DNA from the murder scene as that of a man who had previously served time for molesting a seventeen-year-old girl. Further testing confirmed a match, and the rapist was charged with the crime.[8]

Saliva and DNA

Saliva has proved to be another source of important DNA evidence used in tracking criminals. DNA profiles can be made of saliva left on a stamp, a cigarette butt, or even on the mouthpiece of a telephone. Serial killer Ted Bundy was linked to one of his victims not only by matching bite marks made by Bundy's teeth with bite marks found on the victim's body, but also by matching the DNA in Bundy's saliva to the DNA of the saliva found in the bite marks on the victim.[9]

In May 1995, in one of the largest sting operations ever, more than five thousand police raided eighteen hundred addresses in England and Wales, arresting suspected burglars. The amount of "goods" discovered was huge: thousands of pieces of jewelry, paintings, counterfeit money, drugs, firearms, and one other thing—saliva. Many of those arrested were required to donate mouth saliva to help create a national DNA data bank for Scotland Yard.[10]

DNA Profiling: The Advantages

What makes DNA so valuable in forensic investigation is that a DNA analysis can be made of anything that comes from a living organism. Jim Clark, director of Arkansas's state crime lab, said, "Three to four years down the road, on cases in which we now do serology (blood screens), we will do DNA instead because it is more accurate and scientific."[11] And Carlos Rabren, director of the Alabama Department of Forensic Sciences, said, "DNA is the only biological evidence that says you have the right man or the wrong man. It is the most important evidence for excluding or including suspects."[12]

Establishing Proof of Innocence

What Dr. Rabren said is very important. Some people believe DNA testing is only a tool to prove suspects guilty. Not true. A DNA profile can also prove a suspect innocent. When an intruder raped a Parkville, Maryland, woman, she identified her attacker as a man with whom she had recently ended a four-year relationship. She was sure her ex-boyfriend was the attacker, even though her bedroom was dark during the attack and she did not get a good look at the man.

Police arrested her ex-boyfriend, and while in prison awaiting trial, he met the boyfriend of the victim's roommate. They looked strikingly alike, with the same dark, curly hair and bushy beards. The ex-boyfriend asked detectives to investigate the second man. A DNA profile from the second man matched the DNA in semen samples taken at the crime scene. The second man was the real rapist, and the first man was set free.

Durability

Another advantage of DNA is that it is lasting, whereas genetic markers in blood will disappear after time. Although DNA will deteriorate if exposed to radiation such as sunlight, under proper conditions it can remain intact for centuries. DNA has been extracted from body lice found on Egyptian mummies buried thousands of years ago. The durability of DNA means investigators can reopen cases that occurred before DNA typing was invented and reexamine the evidence, analyzing DNA.

DNA: THE DOWNSIDE

Since the discovery of fingerprinting at the turn of the century, science has played an ever-increasing role in administering justice. To jurors, scientific testimony may carry more weight than eyewitness testimony and is often the deciding factor in juries' verdicts. As one juror said after a trial in Queens, New York, "You can't argue with science."[13] But how can nonscientists evaluate the accuracy of scientific evidence? And whom do they believe when two "expert" scientific witnesses give different opinions regarding evidence?

Some scientific techniques have turned out to be faulty. One example is the paraffin test, which was used by crime laboratories throughout the United States to detect nitrite and nitrate residues from gunpowder on suspects' hands to show they had recently fired a gun. The test was first admitted as scientific evidence in a 1936 trial in Pennsylvania. For the next twenty-five years, many people were convicted by paraffin tests.

Then, in the mid-1960s, a scientific study revealed flaws in the test. In particular, the test gave an unacceptably high number of false positives, meaning substances other than gunpowder were responsible for the nitrate residue on a suspect's hands. These other substances included urine, tobacco, fertilizer, and colored fingernail polish. The result was that many people were convicted of crimes on evidence that later proved to be worthless.[14]

The theory of DNA profiling, stating that no two people, except identical twins, have identical DNA is 100 percent accurate. So DNA profiling in theory is a foolproof method of linking physical evidence to a suspect. Since 1987, DNA analysis has been used in more than one thousand criminal investigations in the United States. But this modern scientific tool, by its very personal and private nature, also has the potential for abuse by unscrupulous investigators who lack the integrity to perform DNA analyses of evidence accurately.

Civil liberties groups voice concern over how DNA profile records are kept, and over how to assure the removal of those records if the accused is acquitted, as is required by law. These groups also express the need for a strict policy code of how, from whom, and when DNA samples for profiling can be obtained. As the law stands now, it is possible for a DNA sample to be taken from a person for a mere driving offense.

GOING FISHING WITH DNA

Another potential for abuse is genetic fishing expeditions using DNA as bait. In such a "fish hunt," many people who have nothing to do with a crime except living in the vicinity of the crime scene would be required to donate tissue samples for DNA profiling. An example is a murder case in Cardiff, Wales. Police there are investigating the 1995 rape and murder of a fifteen-year-old girl, Claire Hood. Her body was found in a woods near the housing project where she lived. One of the few pieces of evidence is the semen of the murderer. Certain that he lives among the eleven thousand residents of the project, the police made a list of around two thousand men and asked them to give blood samples. Those who refuse, says Stuart Lewis, a chief inspector involved in the case, will find themselves under interrogation by the police.

Many people are complaining that this sort of situation amounts to harassment. Advocates of DNA profiling argue that the process can also serve to prevent harassment and false arrest. If you are innocent, they say, you will be eliminated as a suspect. It could also be argued that the law says a person is innocent until proven guilty. And many people feel that the forced DNA testing is also an invasion of a person's natural right to privacy.[15]

DNA Data Banks

Adding to the potential for DNA-testing abuse is the creation of computer files of DNA test results taken from suspects. Once a DNA profile is on file, if the suspect commits another crime and leaves a sample of his cell tissues behind, that sample can be easily matched to his DNA test result in the computer.

If handled with integrity, a DNA data bank could be a welcome addition to the arsenal of crime-fighting weapons used by forensic investigators. However, as Dr. David Werrett, research director of the Forensic Science Service, the agency that will compile the DNA data bank in England, said, "We all get junk mail, and you wonder whose computer your name is on. I think people have a right to raise these issues."[16] The concern is that the DNA profiles of innocent people may be improperly added to, or held in, DNA data banks.

Dr. Werrett also points out that a series of safeguards will be built into the system. Besides mandating the deletion of all DNA data for people who are acquitted or whose charges are dropped, British law gives citizens the right to know whether their DNA profile is in the data bank. Further, like requesting a second opinion from another doctor in a medical diagnosis, if DNA analysts score a hit linking an individual with a crime, police must gather a second sample from the suspect and have it tested at a different laboratory.

Another safeguard for DNA testing is the United States Clinical Laboratories Improvement Act of 1967, which established a system of accreditation and proficiency testing for clinical laboratories that service the medical profession. The law was enacted to insure that those laboratories that are not subject to the same scientific scrutiny as research laboratories would still provide reliable data.

The potential for abuse should not discount the value of DNA testing. If proper procedures are followed, DNA analysis is amazingly accurate. On average, only one in thirty billion people will yield the same DNA profile. And if criminals see how impossible it is to get away with illegal acts due to DNA evidence, perhaps this genetic tool will be the longed-for deterrent that stops the rising crime rate occurring in almost every country in the world. Conducted by honest, intelligent investigators, DNA profiling will more and more often be the clue that cracks the case.

4

NONBIOLOGICAL EVIDENCE

On November 1, 1955, Flight 629 took off from Denver, Colorado's, Stapleton Airport. Eleven minutes later, the plane exploded, killing forty-four people. This was the first major case in which nonbiological evidence played a vital role in tracking down a killer. The FBI sifted through thousands of tiny pieces of wreckage. Some of the pieces were an unusual blackish gray color. When analyzed, forensic chemists discovered these pieces consisted mainly of sodium carbonate, normally found in scouring powder.

The debris was the clue that cracked the case. When dynamite explodes, the heat of the blast frees sodium atoms. Sodium atoms like to combine with other elements, in this case carbon dioxide to form sodium carbonate. The tiny blackish gray particles were the remains of a dynamite explosion. The cause of the plane crash was a bomb.

Flight 629 was the first known case of sabotage in modern aviation history. Tiny pieces of battery wire found in the wreckage were later matched to wire discovered in the home of Jack Gilbert Graham. His motive? Money. His mother was taking that flight, and he had bought several flight insurance policies for her, naming himself as the beneficiary. Graham was convicted and executed in Colorado's gas chamber.[1]

Stop reading a minute, and look around the room you are in. If a crime occurred right now, which things would you expect to become evidence? If you left out something you see in the room, put it back on your list. For anything, absolutely anything, found at the crime scene can become evidence. Biological evidence is only one piece of the puzzle. Examination of nonbiological evidence, or what forensic investigators call materials analysis, plays an equally important role in tracking down the perpetrator.

Nonbiological evidence includes poisons, guns, bullets, knives, explosives, glass, fibers, documents, paint, chemicals, soil, metals, tire treads, and shoe prints, to name just a few examples. Forensic scientists need to know what the evidence is made of, where it came from, who bought it, and who brought it to the crime scene. They hope the answers to those questions will all add up to the thread of evidence that will link the criminal to the crime.

FIREARMS AND BULLETS

Old-time sheriffs used to look for a "smoking gun" to catch a killer, meaning they hoped to catch the criminal with the gun in his hands, with smoke still coming from the barrel. Today forensic experts look for the smoke. Guns leave clues, even if the gun is long gone from the crime scene. A bullet found in a victim can be traced to the gun that fired it, and from the gun, to the killer who pulled the trigger.

The first time bullets were used to link a suspect to a crime was in 1835, when a detective from London's Bow Street Runners, the predecessor to Scotland Yard, matched a ridge mark on a bullet from a victim's body to a ridge mark in a bullet mold in a suspect's home. Confronted with the evidence, the suspect confessed, and the science of ballistics was born.[2]

The first recorded case in America that hinged on ballistic evidence occurred in 1879, when a man was acquitted of murder after it was proved his gun had not been fired in over a year. In a 1902 murder trial, Judge Oliver Wendell Holmes asked a gunsmith to determine if a bullet removed from a victim's body had been fired from a suspect's gun. The gunsmith fired shots from the gun into a basket filled with cotton so that he could retrieve the bullets. He then used a magnifying glass and microscope to show the jury that marks found on the bullet from the victim were identical to marks on the test bullets. This is still the way ballistics tests are conducted today. Bullets fired from the same gun share certain distinctive markings.[3]

RIFLING

What are these marks on bullets? As a group, the marks are called rifling. Individually, these marks consist of grooves, lands, and twists. Spiral grooves carved inside the gun barrel to increase accuracy and range cause a bullet to spin rapidly through the barrel. The raised areas between the grooves are called lands. As a bullet spins down the barrel, these lands and grooves make marks on it. The twist is the direction the spiral makes a bullet spin in, either clockwise or counterclockwise. By measuring the number of lands and grooves, their width, and the direction of the twist on a fired bullet, it is possible to determine what kind of gun fired the bullet. The FBI crime lab maintains a database of firearms riflings from more than eighteen thousand different weapons.

Although rifling can identify the make and model of the weapon fired, in order to identify a specific weapon used in a crime, investigators compare the marks found on the inside of the gun barrel with marks made on a fired bullet. Firearms manufacturers use a sharp tool to cut grooves into gun barrels, and this tool gets worn down microscopically with each cut, thus leaving slightly different marks, called striations, inside the barrel. No two guns will have the same striations.

Other parts of the gun also possess individual characteristics. The firing pin and ejector come into contact with the cartridge case and scar the case with distinctive markings that can be identified with a specific gun. To make ballistic comparisons, experts use the comparison microscope, invented in the 1920s by Phillip O. Gravelle. With this microscope, images formed by two lenses can be viewed side by side through a single lens.[4]

You have probably seen a detective on television pick up a gun at a crime scene by sticking his fountain pen into the barrel. This is not what a real detective would do. Sticking something inside the barrel would destroy identifying marks. The proper way to pick up a gun used in a crime is to pick it up touching only the rough surface of the grip, then drop it into a plastic bag.

SURFACE PROFILE ANALYSIS

In 1993, forensic scientists began using a new technology called surface profile analysis to examine bullet surfaces. A surface profile analyzer is a computerized instrument that scans a bullet and provides a three-dimensional map of the bullet surface. To make the map, the analyzer focuses a laser beam on the bullet, which scans the entire surface. As the light reflects off the projections and depressions made by scratches on the bullet, the computer analyzer graphs the peaks and valleys. When the entire surface has been scanned, the computer creates a three-dimensional representation of the bullet, showing all the scratches in fine detail. The bullet profiles can be entered into a computer database and searched, allowing criminalists to make quick comparisons between the pattern of scratches on a bullet found at a crime scene and the patterns of scratches on bullets fired by various guns.

Besides examining the gun itself, police can also tie a suspect to a shooting by examining the suspect's hands with a technique developed in the 1980s called energy dispersive X-ray analysis. This technique analyzes particles from a suspect's hands for microscopic gunshot residue. The residue is formed when a firearm discharges. When a gun is fired, solid material from the primer, the substance that ignites the cartridge, is liquefied by the high temperatures and pressures created by the igniting gunpowder. Tiny globules of the chemical elements lead, barium, and antimony form while in the liquid state, then immediately cool to become solid spheres.[5]

To determine whether a suspect has recently fired a gun, forensic experts press a piece of tape onto the skin of the suspect to remove any particles. Then a crime technician examines the tape using the scanning electron microscope. The microscope sends a focused beam of electrons across the surface of the particles on the tape. As the electrons strike the particles, they give off X rays, whose energy level depends on the chemical composition of the particles. By analyzing the energy level of the X rays coming from a particular particle, an analyst can determine which elements it contains. In this way, the mix of lead, barium, and antimony in gunshot residue can be distinguished from similar residue that does not come from gunshots, such as lead particles from automobile exhaust, or iron particles from welding processes.[6]

In 1990, energy dispersive X-ray analysis helped determine whether Christian Brando, son of actor Marlon Brando, purposely or accidentally shot and killed his half sister's boyfriend, Dag Drollet. Police claimed Christian had walked up to and shot Drollet as he lay on a couch watching television. Brando insisted the shot had been fired accidentally as the two men struggled over the gun. Gunshot residue found on Drollet's hands proved his hands were on or near the gun when it fired, thus clearing Christian Brando of premeditated murder. He was convicted of the lesser charge of manslaughter.[7]

POISONS

Poisons are another example of nonbiological evidence. Because of the huge number of toxic substances sold over the counter, criminal cases involving poisons are in many ways the most difficult to solve. The first rule of toxicology is "the dose is the poison." In sufficient amounts, anything can be poisonous. Water is poison when someone drowns. Aspirin is fatal in large doses. About 50 percent of all human poisoning cases in the United States involve common household products or over-the-counter drugs, such as aspirin, insecticides, and cosmetics.

In 1982, John Wesley Gentry, of Florida, was rushed to the emergency room. He was treated and sent home, although the cause of his illness was never found. Weeks later, he was again rushed to the hospital with the same symptoms. Every medication he had been taking was analyzed. Capsules in a bottle of Vitamin C given to him by his girlfriend, Judy Buenoaño, turned out not to be Vitamin C at all. Toxicologists broke a capsule down into its individual components to see if it was a polymer, a substance made by linking similar molecules. Sure enough, it was a polymer identified as paraformaldehyde. The chemists had never seen this polymer before, so they started looking for products that paraformaldehyde is contained in.

Meanwhile, investigators discovered that John Gentry had survived another brush with death when a bomb blew up his car. Detectives ran a background check on the only other person close to John, his girlfriend, Judy Buenoaño. They discovered that one of her children from a previous marriage had drowned in a canoeing accident. And that child's father had died mysteriously. She then began dating another man, who also died under questionable circumstances. In addition, detectives learned that Judy had received huge amounts of money from life insurance policies she had taken out on all three victims. But the evidence really pointed to Judy when detectives learned she had taken out a large life insurance policy on John Gentry four months before he entered the hospital for the first time.

Investigator's suspicions paid off when they searched the beauty shop where Judy worked. There they found a bottle labeled "Poison," which contained tablets used to make a disinfectant for brushes and combs. The chemical in the tablets was found to be the mysterious polymer paraformaldehyde. Judy had crushed the tablets into a powder and put the powder into John's vitamin-C capsules. The problem was that she had not used enough to kill him. Judy never learned the first rule of toxicology: the dose is the poison.[8]

THE MASS SPECTROMETER

In order to identify the poison used in a murder, forensics experts must separate the poison from other chemicals found in the victim's body. To do this, toxicologists use a technique called chromatography, which separates components of a mixture. Tissue samples are taken from the victim's vital organs, blood, or urine. Extractions are performed to separate poisons from other body fluids. Then, to identify the chemicals in the poisons, an instrument called a mass spectrometer, or mass spec, for short, is used. The mass spec can identify chemicals from the most minute tissue samples.

Every chemical has unique properties, meaning each chemical consists of a different combination of the basic elements. Forensic toxicologists use the mass spec to identify every chemical present in the unknown chemical sample. Then the chemicals identified are compared to known chemical substances. Thus, the mass spec provides a chemical "fingerprint."

In 1982, a new kind of crime emerged in the United States: product tampering. The first product known to be tampered with was Tylenol. Seven people in Chicago, Illinois, died after taking Tylenol tablets laced with potassium cyanide, a fast-acting poison that kills by blocking oxygen from blood cells.

Although the person who poisoned the Tylenol was never caught, investigators learned valuable techniques from this case that have been used in other product-tampering cases. Because potassium absorbs X rays, potassium cyanide would show up on an X ray. But how could investigators X-ray thousands of Tylenol bottles quickly? The answer was found at the airport. FBI agents put the bottles through X-ray machines used to screen luggage.[9]

AN EXCEDRIN HEADACHE   In 1986, a Seattle, Washington, woman, Sue Snow, took two capsules of Extra-Strength Excedrin. She died within minutes. When the assistant medical examiner performed an autopsy, she smelled bitter almonds, the recognized smell of cyanide, a poison that keeps oxygen from the blood stream. Tissue samples from Sue Snow were found to contain cyanide.

Police collected Excedrin bottles in Washington and four other states. Using an airport X-ray machine, two more bottles of poisoned Excedrin were discovered. Toxicologists found specks of green material in the poisoned capsules. All except 1 percent of the green specks consisted of sodium chloride, table salt, used in many products to add bulk and carry the active chemical ingredients. The 1 percent was found to contain four chemicals, two of which were algicides, products that kill algae in fish aquariums.

Investigators examined fish tank cleaners at pet stores to find a product that contained all four of the green speck chemicals. Bingo. They found the chemicals in an algicide named Algae Destroyer. And the tablets in Algae Destroyer were the same green color as the specks found in the Excedrin tablets.

Meanwhile, another person, Bruce Nickell, also of Seattle, died from taking poisoned Extra-Strength Excedrin. Investigators discovered that Bruce Nickell's wife, Stella, had a fish tank in her trailer. From then on, the evidence against Stella mounted. A clerk in a pet store remembered selling her a package of Algae Destroyer and a mortar and pestle to mash the tablets. Her fingerprints were found on several books about poisons she checked out of a library.

When questioned further, she admitted her husband died a week before Sue Snow. Investigators discovered she had taken out three accidental death life insurance policies on her husband the previous year, totaling $175,000. Insurance companies consider death by poisoning to be accidental. Further, her husband's signature on two of the insurance policies had been forged.

Stella Nickell was the killer in the Excedrin case. The true story unfolded like this: Stella Nickell started out to kill only one person, but when the coroner mistakenly ruled her husband's death due to natural causes, not an accident, she was not entitled to the life insurance money. Therefore, she had to kill others to get the coroner to notice the poisoned Excedrin capsules. Stella Nickell became the first person convicted of murder in a product-tampering case. She is currently serving a ninety-year prison sentence.[10]

DRUG CASES

Because drugs given in sufficient amounts are poisons, too, the Chem/Tox Unit of a forensic laboratory also handles drug cases. To identify a drug in a victim, toxicologists separate it from other chemicals found in samples of the victim's blood, urine, or body fluids. In one case, a gruesome evidence package was sent to the

FBI lab from Houston, Texas: a chain saw and a woman's head. She had been raped and murdered, and her body had been cut up with a chain saw. Police knew her identity, but wanted to confirm an informant's claim that she had taken large amounts of cocaine shortly before her death.

Sometimes when a body is decomposed, the only body fluid available to test for drugs is the liquid from the eyes, called the aqueous humor, because this liquid does not decompose. The lab confirmed high amounts of cocaine in the eye liquid. Police used this information to link the victim to a drug party that had gotten out of hand. Detectives traced the murder to a man who was at the party.

DRUG SMUGGLING

Drug smuggling has become the most common of all major crimes. Chemists working for drug dealers add liquefied cocaine to other chemicals used to make plastic, then mold the plastic into common items. Once the items have cleared customs at an airport or pier, the chemists can reverse the process, liquefying the items to extract the cocaine. Plastic items implanted with cocaine have included fiberglass bathtubs, dog kennels, and plastic plumbing fixtures.

Drug-sniffing dogs and chemical tests cannot find drugs being smuggled this way. To solve the problem, toxicologists use an ion spectrometer, an instrument originally developed by NASA (National Aeronautics and Space Administration) to analyze alien atmospheres. As modified for use in law enforcement, this instrument vacuums particles off the surface of an object and determines within four seconds if a drug is present.

SOIL

Common dirt provides still another example of nonbiological evidence. Mineral analyses of soil can reveal differences in its composition. From soil samples, forensic scientists can tell whether the soil was close to a road, near a building, how close it was to fresh or salt water, what plant and animal life might be found nearby, whether the area was urban or rural, and whether the soil had been fertilized. Soil analysis can also give information about the victims in crimes.

When the bodies of Drug Enforcement Agency (DEA) agent Kiki Camarena and the pilot who helped him discover marijuana plantations near Guadalajara, Mexico, were discovered on a dirt road, soil evidence proved the men had been buried elsewhere first, then moved to the dirt road. The bodies were covered with dark soil, but the dirt they were lying on was light gray. More about this case in the next chapter.

METALS

Examination of metal material found at crime scenes can provide identification of the source of an item. Metal experts, called metallurgists, can determine if two similar broken items were once a whole item, the force causing the breakage, the direction from which the force came, and the time when the fragments became separated. Metallurgical examinations can also determine how a metal item was manufactured, and whether items found in different locations were made at the same time and by the same manufacturer. Another important crime-detecting task of the metallurgist is to restore erased, altered, or scratched-off code numbers from items such as automobiles, jewelry, and license plates.

DOCUMENT EXAMINATIONS

Document examination includes comparing questioned handwriting with known handwriting samples to determine a writer's identity. The Document Unit in a forensic lab examines forgeries, typewriting, inks, paper, rubber-stamp impressions, and charred paper.

No two people write the same, even identical twins. In fact, no one can write his or her own signature exactly the same way twice. Try it. Write your name on two separate pieces of paper, then lay one over the other and hold them up to a light. One will never exactly match the other.

You have probably received a letter in the mail and knew just by looking at your name on the envelope who wrote it because you recognized the handwriting. Examination of handwriting samples works much the same way. Experts look at many samples of an individual's normal writing, then compare the writing style on a questioned document to those samples. Peculiarities will always be found, and these peculiarities form the basis for an expert's opinion as to who wrote a questioned document. The peculiarities examiners look for include the size and height of the letters, their slant, how far above or below the line letters are formed, the distance between words, and the way *is* are dotted and *ts* are crossed.

THE LINDBERGH KIDNAPPING

Perhaps the first major case in which handwriting analysis played a role in finding the criminal was the 1932 kidnapping and murder of Charles and Anne Morrow Lindbergh's baby son. More than two years after the body was found, a man named Bruno Richard Hauptmann was caught after spending some of the ransom money. Although other circumstantial evidence linked Hauptmann to the kidnapping, it was his handwriting that convinced a jury of his guilt. A sample of Hauptmann's handwriting was compared to the handwriting on the ransom notes. The handwriting expert, Charles Appel, testified at a grand jury hearing that he had examined fifteen hundred different handwriting samples without finding any of the same peculiarities he found in both Hauptmann's writing and the writing on the ransom notes. Bruno Hauptmann was convicted of the crime. He always swore he was innocent, and his conviction remains one of the most controversial jury verdicts in American history.[11]

PAINT

Any substance found at a crime scene can be used to place a suspect at the crime scene by matching that substance to the same substance found on a suspect. And one of the most valuable substances found at crime scenes is paint, one of the most commonly encountered man-made substances in the world. When paint is found at a crime scene, forensic experts attempt to discover what it is made of and where it was manufactured. A collection of paint sample analyses have been accumulated in many large police departments' computer databases throughout the country. The largest is the FBI's National Automotive Paint File, begun in 1932, which today contains a computer database of more than forty thousand original paint finish samples.

To begin an analysis, the forensic expert will compare the paint sample from the crime scene with those in the databases. To discover where a particular paint sample was made, its chemical makeup is analyzed. For example, if a speck of white paint is found at a crime scene, forensic scientists know that white paint is not just white paint. It is composed of organic and inorganic pigments to give it color, solvents that carry the pigments, a binder to hold the paint to a surface, and additives to make the paint waterproof, shiny, or long-lasting. An analysis of the chemical makeup of a paint sample can prove that one sample of white paint is different from all other samples of white paint. That information, plus the fact that paint can be transferred from one object to another—from the victim to a suspect, for example—makes paint a most valuable clue when found at a crime scene.

In September 1984, in Flowing Wells, Arizona, eight-year-old Vicki Hoskinson went for a ride on her pink bicycle and disappeared. The bicycle was found lying in the street, its frame damaged. Seven months later, some of Vicki's remains, along with her crushed skull, were found in the Arizona desert. The first break in the case came when a jailed convict claimed that a fellow prisoner named Frank Jarvis Atwood told him he had bumped a little girl off her bicycle with his car, taken her into the desert, sexually molested her, then strangled her and beat her to death with a large rock. Without physical evidence linking Atwood to the crime scene, the defense could claim the informant made up the story to get a shorter sentence for himself. So forensic experts attempted to prove that Atwood's car, which was in police custody, had hit Vicki Hoskinson's bike.

Both the bicycle and Frank Atwood's car bumper were submitted to the crime lab. Specks of pink paint, no larger than the dot over an *i*, found on the bumper were identical to the paint on the bicycle. The way the forensic expert determined the match was to take a scraping of the paint found on Atwood's bumper and put it in a pyrolysis gas chromatograph mass spectrometer. This instrument burns a sample at 760 degrees Centigrade, in order to separate and chart the gases released by a substance as its compounds are vaporized. The chart provides a detailed analysis of the chemical makeup of a sample. The same process was performed on a scraping of the pink paint from Vicki's bike.

Next, both samples were examined under a scanning electron microscope to identify the metallic elements present in the paint. If there had been a transfer of paint from the bicycle to the bumper, there also might have been a transfer of the bumper's nickel coating to the bicycle. In three different places on the bicycle, the microscope detected traces of nickel similar to the nickel plating on the bumper. When this evidence was presented in court, the jury found Frank Atwood guilty of murdering Vicki Hoskinson, and he was sentenced to death.[12]

Paint also plays a major role in solving hit-and-run accidents, as paint is often the only evidence found at the scene of these crimes. Paint chips have been found embedded in victims' clothes, on their eyeglasses or belt buckles, in their shoes, under their fingernails, and even on their false teeth. Almost no chip is too small to be a clue. Forensic experts have a rule that if you can see it, you can work with it. From the FBI's National Automotive Paint File, or paint file databases in other police departments, forensic chemists can identify the year, make, and model of a car by comparing the physical characteristics and chemical composition of paint found at a crime scene with that of known specimens. Paint and automobile manufacturers routinely provide the FBI with information for their computer database.

FOOTPRINTS

Like fingerprints, footprints are one of the oldest methods of catching criminals. Shoe impressions are found at almost every crime scene. Although shoes come in many different styles, footwear comparisons can be narrowed down to a specific shoe, based on design, size, shape, and normal wear of the shoe. This wear and tear can include important clues, such as a nail embedded in the heel, gum stuck to the toe, or a pebble wedged into the sole—all of which make one shoe stand out from all the other shoes in the world.

When footprints are found at crime scenes, either from shoes or bare feet, if the criminal wore no shoes, investigators photograph them. Then, if it is a depression (a shoe print made deep into soft material such as mud), a plaster cast is made of the print. If a photograph will not provide enough detail, or if a cast cannot be made, investigators attempt to lift that section of surface where the footprint is found. The FBI's forensic lab has been sent entire floors, countertops, staircases, and kitchen sinks with footprints on them.

Like latent fingerprints, invisible footprints can be enhanced with chemicals or powder, then lifted with tape. When a woman who managed a New York City Gap store was murdered, a slab of concrete flooring and tile were sent to a forensic lab, where technicians enhanced a barely visible athletic-shoe print made in her blood. That impression was matched to a sneaker worn by a former employee and led to his conviction.[13]

For footprints found in dust, which could be blown away by the smallest breeze, a new tool called an electrostatic duster comes to the rescue. This is how it works. A sheet of black lifting material is laid over the surface of the footprint, and a high-voltage charge is run through the material. Just as clothes taken out of a dryer pop with "electricity" and cling together, the electric charge draws the material down tightly against the surface, and the dust is transferred to the lifter. The foot impression is actually made by the dust itself.

TIRE PRINTS

Tire tread impressions are almost as useful as footprints in tracking criminals. There are thousands of tread designs, and every tire wears differently. Forensic scientists can identify a specific make of tire from a tread impression and often find the exact tire that left the impression. The FBI, for example, regularly updates its database of tread designs from tire manufacturers. Further, since most people do not replace all four tires at the same time, the combination of tire tread marks found at crime scenes makes strong evidence that a particular car was present at the scene. In addition, tires pick up debris from the road. So by analyzing debris found in tire treads, investigators may be able to place that car at a crime scene.

In one case, Florida police searching for a serial killer knew the man was driving a sedan with two unusual rear tires, one of which was put on so the whitewall faced inward. When Bobby Joe Long was identified as a suspect, an examination of the tires on his car proved it had been used in at least two murders.

Tire impressions are often found on the bodies of hit-and-run victims. As a car runs over a body, clothing wraps around the tire, so that the imprint of the sidewall, the part of the tire on which the brand name and model number appear, is sometimes pressed into the cloth. This information can lead police to the hit-and-run driver's vehicle, and to the driver as well.

GLASS

People think of glass as extremely fragile. The truth is glass is one of the hardest substances in the world—even harder than steel. But glass does break easily, and broken glass is a highly valuable clue to detectives. This is because while glass may shatter into thousands of fragments, each fragment will have the same color, density, and refractive index. The refractive index is a measurement of the angle at which a straight path of light becomes deflected, or bent, when shined through the glass. So when broken glass is found at a crime scene, scientists measure these three properties.

When committing a crime, the perpetrator often breaks a window in order to enter a locked house or building. When you break glass, such as a windowpane, tiny shards of glass land on the floor, your hair, clothing, and the soles of your shoes—without your being aware of it. Moreover, these slivers stay there for a very long time, and will probably still be there even after washing your clothes or sweeping the floor. Thus, if glass shards are found on a suspect, these same three properties of the glass—color, density, and the refractive index—are measured to see if they match the glass found at the crime scene. If they do, the suspect can be placed at the crime scene.

When a serial rapist dove through the window of a victim's house to escape, samples of glass shards from the window, his clothing, and a pair of leather gloves he was wearing when caught were examined. The lab found a match between the window glass and glass found on the suspect. In the suspect's clothes, they also found glass that had not come from that window. Police went back to other houses where the rapist had gained entry by smashing a window. Although the broken glass had been replaced, by wiping down the windowsills with a damp cloth, they found fragments that matched the glass found on the suspect, thus linking him to the other rapes as well.[14]

Glass can also be found embedded in tools used to smash into homes or buildings. Weeks after a mass murder in Georgia, a boy found a .22-Magnum gun while fishing in a pond. A firearms examiner noticed several long scratches on the gun barrel. Tiny bits of glass were found in the scratches. To gain entry into the victims' home, the killer had smashed a window-pane with an unknown object. Even though the gun had lain at the bottom of a pond for weeks, the glass was still there. A match was found between those slivers and broken glass from the victims' back door. When the gun was traced back to its owner, he pled guilty to murder and was sentenced to life in prison.

BULLETS AND GLASS

When bullets are fired through glass, forensic experts can examine the glass fragments to learn three things about a crime: which side of the glass the shooter was standing on; the angle from which the bullet was fired; and the sequence in which the bullets were fired if more than one shot was fired.

Most people think when someone shoots through glass, the broken pieces will fall away from the shooter. Wrong. Glass is elastic, and when an object goes through it, glass will bend, then snap back, an occurrence called blowback. Glass will blow back a maximum of eighteen feet. By examining glass particles found on a suspect's clothing, police have been able to place the suspect between twelve and eighteen feet from a piece of glass.

It is also possible to figure out where the shooter was standing by determining the angle at which the bullet hit the glass. If the bullet hole is round, the bullet was fired at a right angle to the glass, meaning the shooter was standing directly in front of it. As the angle of the shooter to the glass increases, the bullet hole will become more and more elongated.

Knowing the order in which bullets were fired through glass is especially useful to investigators when a suspect says someone else fired at him first, and he fired back in self-defense. Usually, when a bullet is fired through tempered glass—glass that is toughened by a process of gradual heating and cooling—or through glass that is held securely in a frame, the glass cracks but does not shatter. Long thin cracks, like a spider web, stretch out from each bullet hole. Each crack stretches out until it meets another crack.

So, the first shot fired will cause many uninterrupted cracks. The cracks created by the second shot will end wherever they cross paths with cracks from the first shot; cracks created by the third shot will stop when they meet cracks from either of the first two shots, and so on. Once two or more bullet holes are put in sequence, the size of the hole, the angle of the shot, and the gunpowder residue found around the hole unlock the secret of which gun fired what bullet.[15]

ARSON

The Document Section of a forensic laboratory handles certain cases of arson, the deliberate setting of a fire, in which paper products are evidence. And matches made of paper are often found at fires in which arson is suspected. The goal of the arson investigator is to connect the matches with a suspect.

Every paper match has little particles sticking out of its side. That is because paper matches are produced from fillers consisting of everything from rag threads to paint chips. These particles fit perfectly with adjoining matches in the same matchbook, but not with matches from another matchbook. When burned-out matches are examined under a microscope, if the two sides do not fit, they did not come from the same matchbook. When burned matches were found near the place where a suspicious fire had started in California's Los Padres National Forest, investigators linked the matches to a matchbook found on a suspect. A forensic documents expert showed that the ragged edges of the burned matches fit together perfectly with the ragged edges of the matches still left in the matchbook.[16]

Criminals who are careful not to leave fingerprints often leave other incriminating evidence behind. A chip of paint, a mark on a bullet, the cracks in a windowpane, the chemicals in a bottle of aspirin, or the way someone crosses his *t*s or dots his *i*s sometimes turns out to be the thread of evidence that keeps a criminal from getting away with the perfect crime.

5

HAIRS AND FIBERS

In February 1985, DEA agent Kiki Camarena and his pilot, Alfredo Zavala, located several large marijuana plantations outside Guadalajara. The Mexican government, which was taking bribes to keep quiet about the crop, reluctantly had no choice but to destroy it. The marijuana had an estimated value of $3 billion. Not long afterward, Camarena and Zavala were kidnapped. Two Mexican drug traffickers, Rafael Caro-Quintero and Ernesto Fonseca, were the prime suspects.

However, because the suspects' drug organization was paying huge bribes to the Mexican government to keep quiet about their marijuana business, Mexican officials made it extremely difficult for the DEA investigators to develop any evidence against them. In retaliation, the United States government exerted economic pressure on the Mexican government to cooperate. Every car entering Mexico from San Diego, California, was searched thoroughly, discouraging tourist travel to Mexico, a big industry there. In addition, the long lines of cars waiting to enter Mexico at the border included trucks carrying fresh produce, which rotted in the trucks.

The Mexican police (the MFJP) learned Camarena and Zavala were being held at a ranch owned by the Bravo drug gang, rivals to the Caro-Quintero operation. A joint raid by the MFJP and the DEA was scheduled. But the MFJP lied about the time of the raid and got there first. They killed the entire Bravo gang. Two days later, the bodies of Camarena and Zavala were found lying on a road on the ranch, wrapped in plastic bags.

An FBI forensic team went to investigate. The first lead was a light beige nylon carpet fiber found on Zavala's sweatshirt. That fiber meant Zavala had been in contact with a light beige rug. An informant told DEA agents that one of Fonseca's gang members had parked a brand new car in his brick garage, then bricked up the door, in effect burying the car. When the brick was torn down, a new Mercury Marquis was found in the garage. And on the car's rear floor was found a single hair. The hair was matched to Camarena. In April, the MFJP claimed to have evidence that Camarena and Zavala had been held in a villa in downtown Guadalajara, owned by Rafael Caro-Quintero.

When FBI agents were finally allowed inside, the house had been cleaned and every wall repainted. A squad of MFJP officers was stationed in the house, supposedly to protect the crime scene, but in reality they were there to confiscate any evidence the FBI found. However, in their haste to rid the house of incriminating evidence, the MFJP overlooked a vital clue—a light beige nylon carpet, installed in an unattached guest house just before Camarena and Zavala were kidnapped. And in that carpet were found two head hairs. The hairs matched hair samples from Kiki Camarena. When the fibers found on Zavala's sweatshirt were matched to the carpet fibers in the guest house, forensic investigators knew that both men had been in that room. Then two more of Camarena's head hairs were found in a car parked next to the house, suggesting that he had been transported in both the Mercury Marquis and that car to or from the villa.

The Mexican government had tried to erase all clues from the crime scene in order to lead United States investigators away from the Caro-Quintero gang. They removed the bodies from their original grave at the villa and took them to the Bravo gang's ranch, thereby focusing attention on the rival gang as the killers. But hairs and fibers are so small and often overlooked that getting rid of every single one is almost impossible. Kiki Camarena and Alfredo Zavala had been held, and most likely killed, at the villa. The Mexican government did not remember the first rule of forensic investigation: a person always carries something of himself to a place, and takes something on his person *away* from that place. In this case, "something" was two small hairs and beige carpet fibers.[1]

Because hairs can be either human, as in head hairs, or synthetic, as in fibers from a wig, hairs and fibers are grouped together in forensic investigations. Hairs and fibers have been used to link criminals with their crimes for over 150 years. The first known case of hairs as evidence in America occurred in Massachusetts in 1869, when hairs found stuck to the dried blood on the end of a club helped convict a man of beating his wife to death.[2]

Today the FBI forensic lab holds a hair collection that includes samples from every part of the body, from every race of people, and from almost every animal in existence. The largest and toughest hair in the collection is from an elephant. And that hair has really been used to convict people who break the law. When anyone charged with illegally bringing elephant hair bracelets into the country claims the material in their bracelet is synthetic, all forensic scientists have to do is compare a single hair from the tourist's bracelet to the very real elephant hair in the lab's collection.

HAIRS TELL STORIES

A single hair tells volumes of information. Forensic scientists can learn from that single hair whether it came from an animal or a human; whether it was Caucasoid, Negroid, or Mongoloid; what part of the body it came from; how long ago the hair was dyed or bleached; and whether the person suffered from certain diseases, or used a specific drug. Forensic scientists can tell if a hair has been forcibly removed. In that case, the root will be elongated rather than round. Torn out hair may also have skin tissue still attached, and will contain pigment all the way down to the tip of the root, because it was still in the root stage when pulled out.

It is not possible, however, to tell whether the hair came from a man or woman, or the age of the person whose hair is found when comparing hairs in forensic science. Forensic scientists use only head, pubic, and facial hairs in criminal investigations, as there is not enough difference between two people's body hairs to make a good comparison.

Every hair has a combination of characteristics that makes it different from others—length, color, curliness or straightness, texture, thickness, diameter of the hair shaft, shape and condition of the root, and the presence of dyes or bleaches. There are also internal characteristics that make each hair different from others, such as the width of the medulla (the core running down the center of a hair); the type and condition of the scales that make up the cuticle, or outer layers; and the size, shape, and density of the pigment, which gives hair its color. These differences are what forensic scientists look for when making comparisons between a suspect's hair and hair found on a victim, or at a crime scene.

Foreign material found on hairs, such as dirt and lice, also allows forensic examiners to connect a suspect to a crime. When a woman was murdered by a bullet fired at close range, a bluish material was found in her hair. The suspect in the case had a semiautomatic weapon under the front seat of his car when he was arrested. The first round in that gun was an unusual type of ammunition called a glaser round. This is a bullet with a Teflon shell that disintegrates upon impact and releases small pellets. Tests confirmed that the bluish material in the victim's hair was Teflon that had stuck to the hair on impact. Thus a strong connection was made between the suspect and victim.

Hairs can also be found on weapons used to hit the victim, proving a certain weapon, such as a hammer, was the instrument used to commit the crime.

HAIRS IDENTIFY VICTIMS AND CRIMINALS

Hairs can also be examined to identify bodies. When the space shuttle *Challenger* exploded shortly after liftoff in 1986, hairs recovered from the wreckage were one means of identifying the bodies.

By comparing hairs from the crime scene to hairs on a suspect, hairs can be linked to one specific person, and therefore provide extremely strong evidence in crimes. Criminals know this, and sometimes try to disguise or remove their hair before investigators can examine it. Thus, the courts have ruled that law enforcement officials have the right to remove hair samples from suspects without their permission. Suspects have actually been prevented from shaving their heads, getting a haircut, or dyeing their hair until after samples of their hair have been removed.[3]

FIBERS

In March 1975, a fifteen-year-old Michigan girl disappeared and was never seen alive again. She had been about to testify against two men with whom she had been involved in a bad-check scam.

In April, one of the two men was sentenced to prison for an

unrelated crime. Ten years later, the other man claimed the first man had strangled the girl in his car, shot her in the head, then buried her somewhere in the woods. On the basis of his testimony, the first man, out of prison by now, was convicted of murdering the girl.

The first man appealed, claiming the second man killed her. According to his story, in August 1975, while he himself was in prison, the second man threw the girl off a railroad trestle onto rocks below, then buried her in the area. He even told authorities where her body had been buried. Her skeletal remains were found exactly where he said. There was no bullet hole in her head. But the absence of gunshot wounds still did not prove who killed her.

Which man was telling the truth? Another difference in their conflicting stories was the month the murder occurred— March or August. Scraps of the victim's decayed clothing and several pounds of soil found at the grave site were submitted to the FBI forensic lab for testing. The girl had been buried in a swampy area, where there would normally be hordes of insects in August, but not in March, when the ground would be frozen. Further, if the scraps of clothing proved to be winter clothes, she had probably been buried in March, not August. Laboratory tests showed there was no insect activity in the soil, and that the girl had been wearing heavy clothing. The first man was the murderer.[4]

Stop a minute and look at the clothes you are wearing. Somewhere on your clothes you will find some very small fibers. Pick one of these fibers off your clothes and hold it in your hand. It is practically weightless. You probably did not even know it was there. But inside that fiber there exists a world of information.

A thread from an article of clothing becomes a literal "thread of evidence" in many crimes. For example, a fiber found on a slashed window screen at the scene of a break-in may be linked with a suspect's jacket. A thread from a pair of pants found on a suspected car in a hit-and-run case may be linked to the pants the victim was wearing.

When Sherlock Holmes searched for fibers at a crime scene, he whipped out his magnifying glass. If the famous detective were solving crimes today, however, he would probably use a hand-held vacuum cleaner to trap fibers in a special filter. The bits of material he collected might allow him to connect the murder victim to a place, to other victims, or to the killer.

ATLANTA'S SERIAL KILLER

Fibers found on victims of an Atlanta, Georgia, serial killer led directly to the killer's arrest. During a twenty-two-month period, beginning in July 1979, thirty African-American children and young men either disappeared or were murdered around Atlanta. On several of the victims' clothing were found greenish yellow and violet acetate fibers. Forensic investigators knew this meant the victims had all been in the same environment either just prior to or after their deaths. The fibers were identified as carpet fibers.

Before the 1950s, there was little variation in natural fibers and their colors. If a green carpet fiber were found on a victim, like those found on the victims of Wayne Williams, the suspect in the Atlanta killings, there were millions of people who owned the same kind of green carpet. So there was little chance of linking that fiber to a suspect. But after World War II, synthetic fibers were developed in many variations and colors. The manufacture of synthetics made it possible for investigators to now take that same green carpet fiber found on a victim, find out who manufactured it, and narrow down the number of people who could own that exact type and color of green carpet.

After showing the fibers found on the Atlanta victims to carpet manufacturers across the country, agents identified the manufacturer of the fibers as the Wellman Corporation, a Massachusetts company. Yarn made from this fiber, called 181B, had been sold to West Point Pepperell, a Dalton, Georgia, carpet company. Pepperell had used 181B yarn to produce its Luxaire line. Among the colors it had produced was English Olive, a greenish yellow identical to the color of the carpet fibers found on the victims. Sales records showed that only 82 carpets (1 in every 7,792 carpets sold) of this color and type could be expected to be found in all of Georgia.

But just before the FBI located the carpet manufacturer, an Atlanta newspaper printed a story about the unique fibers. The next victim of the serial killer was found nude in the Chatta-hoochee River, having been thrown off a bridge and into the river so the water would wash any hairs and fibers off the body. An FBI team began staking out bridges over the river. About two o'clock one morning, two policemen heard a loud splash. They stopped the only car on the bridge at that time. The driver, an African-American music promoter named Wayne Williams, told police he had just dropped some garbage into the river. Two days later, another young man was found floating in the river. A greenish yellow carpet fiber was found in his hair.

When police searched Williams's house, they found he owned an English Olive Luxaire carpet. Greenish yellow fibers were found in his hair. Carpet fibers found in Williams's car matched those found on the body of the most recent victim. The likelihood of another car with the same carpeting was 1 in 3,828. Thus the probability of victims carrying fibers from both Williams's bedroom carpet and his car carpet was 1 in 29,827,776 (1 in 7,792 x 1 in 3,828). Wayne Williams was arrested and brought to trial. The jury believed these statistics were enough to find him guilty of murder beyond a reasonable doubt. He was convicted of the multiple murders.[5]

ANIMAL, VEGETABLE, OR MINERAL

There are four types of fibers: animal, such as wool; vegetable, such as cotton; mineral, such as asbestos; and man-made or synthetic, such as acrylics, nylon, polyester, and rayon, used in the production of about 75 percent of all clothing. The main characteristics of fibers used to make forensic comparisons are color type, diameter, coarseness, the presence of additives used in production, machine marks made during processing, changes due to use, such as sun bleaching or discoloration, and cross-sectional shape. Artificial fibers are made by forcing molten liquid through a spinneret, a device that looks like a showerhead. So the cross-sectional shape is determined by the shape of the holes in the spinneret.

Perhaps the most important characteristic for forensic investigators is color. For example, a color is produced by mixing various dyes. The amount of these different dyes is determined by an instrument called a microspectrophotometer, which produces a "fingerprint" of the color based on the absorption of light. Identical color "fingerprints" make a strong basis for associating two fibers found in different places. Most comparisons of fibers are done on either a compound microscope, which magnifies a sample up to four hundred times, or the comparison microscope. Every characteristic that is tested for must be the same for a match to be made. If even one difference in characteristics is seen, the two specimens are not the same.[6]

FIBER CLUES FOR CRIME

There is no such thing as a perfect crime. The clues are all there if investigators look carefully enough. For example, if a woman's body is found in a ditch at the side of a road, forensic investigators can look at hairs and fibers found on or near the body and discover where she was when she died, whom she was with, and how she got to this ditch. When these questions are answered, other mysteries will also be solved, such as the race of the person she was with; if she was in a car, house, or on a carpeted surface before being left in the ditch; and if the carpet was old or new. Forensic scientists can also tell if she had a pet, and if so, whether it was a dog, cat, or an exotic animal.

Among the most compelling evidence against serial killer Ted Bundy were ninety-eight cross-transfers of fibers found on Bundy and a twelve-year-old victim, Kimberly Leach. Fibers from Bundy's coat and from the carpet of a van he had stolen were found on Kimberly's clothing, while fibers from her clothing were found on Bundy's clothes. This convinced the jury that Bundy had been in close contact with Kimberly Leach, and helped convict him.[7]

The use of hairs and fibers as evidence is based on French criminologist Dr. Edmond Locard's 1910 theory of transfer. His theory states that when a person comes into contact with another person or place, some fibers and human hair will be transferred to that person and that place. The theory states also that these hairs and fibers are easily shed, so if found on an individual, they will reflect the most recent contact between the individual and another person or place.

In most cases, when this connection is made, the hair or fiber match only becomes important in getting a conviction if the suspect has denied having any contact with the person who was the source of the hairs or the place that was the source of the fibers that were found. For if there is a legitimate reason for the suspect to have been at the crime scene, or if the suspect and the victim are known to have been in contact, then any hairs and fibers found at the crime scene belonging to the suspect would have been expected to be there.

For example, suppose Jim Smith was found shot to death in the men's room at the McDonald's on Elm Street. Detectives find a fiber from Jim Smith's hunting jacket in a suspect's car. And near the toilet in the McDonald's men's room, detectives find a strand of hair matching the suspect's. If the suspect said he and Jim Smith were good friends, and often at the McDonald's on Elm Street, the jury might buy the suspect's claim of innocence in the murder. But if the suspect denies knowing Jim Smith, or ever being at the McDonald's on Elm Street, the jury is going to find it hard to believe the suspect is innocent.

The objective of forensic investigators is to link fibers and hairs from an unknown source to a known source, and then figure out how that connection took place. It is this last objective that requires the most detecting skill.

A CHRISTMAS MURDER SOLVED

On December 3, 1989, five-year-old Melissa Brannen disappeared from a Christmas party in Fairfax, Virginia. A man named Cal Hughes had left the party at the same time. When police arrived at Hughes's home to question him, he was washing the clothes he had worn at the party, an odd thing to do at one in the morning. Hughes became the prime suspect.

Detectives searched his car for fingerprints and bloodstains, and removed the floor mats for testing. They swiped transparent tape over car seats, picking up thousands of hairs and fibers, searching for evidence that Melissa had been in that car. Because tiny hairs and fibers can easily be shed and lost, the evidence is taken into a sealed scraping room and hung on a rack. A clean sheet of white paper is laid under the evidence, and a technician scrapes it with a metal spatula. The hairs and fibers that fall on the white paper are examined under a microscope to match hairs and fibers found in different places.

Melissa had been wearing a blue sweater, and several blue acrylic fibers were found in Hughes's car. In addition, when detectives examined clothes in Melissa's room, several short black hairs were found on one of her nightshirts. They were black rabbit hairs. Melissa had worn a dyed black rabbit coat to the party. The hairs found on Melissa's nightshirt, known to have come from her coat, were compared to hairs found in Hughes's car. They were identical. That match sounds like enough evidence to convict Hughes on the spot. Not so fast. A defense attorney could argue that Hughes had picked up those hairs by accidentally brushing against Melissa at the party.

To prove Melissa had been in that car, the investigator had to link the clothes she was wearing when she disappeared to the debris recovered from the front seat of the car—a seemingly impossible job without having the actual clothes Melissa had worn. The investigator decided to recreate the clothes she was wearing the night she disappeared—red tights, a red plaid skirt, and a blue sweater with a picture of Big Bird on it. The clothes had been given to Melissa by her grandmother, but she could not remember where she bought them.

Pure luck came into play at this point. The investigator was discussing the case with his wife, who remembered an old J. C. Penney catalogue she had saved that featured children's clothing. In the catalogue was a picture of the outfit. It had been manufactured only for J. C. Penney, and it was only advertised in this one catalogue. If the investigator's wife had not kept the catalogue, the case might never have been solved.

The investigator contacted J. C. Penney, and they obtained one of the outfits from a customer in another state. "I'll never forget that night," the investigator said. "As soon as I looked at the fibers under the microscope, I knew we had a match. They were the same fibers we'd found in the car."[8]

Red cotton fibers found on the driver's seat were matched to the red cotton in the skirt. There was no doubt Melissa Brannen had been in Hughes's car, but investigators still had to prove it to a jury. There are more than one thousand man-made fibers currently manufactured, and more than seven thousand different dyes. So the chances that two dyed synthetic fibers from different sources would match are almost zero.

The investigator thought of a dramatic way to show a jury the forensic team's conclusions. Workers in the forensic lab brought in any blue acrylic clothing they owned. A total of 7,938 comparisons were made of 126 different blue acrylic fibers, all from different people. No two fibers could be matched under the microscope. Cal Hughes's statement that he had not spoken to Melissa or been with her was a lie. Hughes was convicted of abduction with intent to harm and received a fifty-year sentence. A tragic postscript to the case is that Hughes never admitted to the abduction, and therefore investigators never learned what happened to Melissa.[9]

There are only three ways to solve a crime. The person who committed the crime can confess; the victim or witnesses can identify the person who committed the crime; or information can be obtained through physical evidence that can be used to link a specific person to the crime or to the victim. The last way is how crimes are solved most often.

Hard evidence is the silent witness. And many times that evidence comes from hairs and fibers, either the criminal's or the victim's. A tiny blue acrylic sweater fiber or one thin black head hair may not seem like much when first looking at a crime scene, but it is just such tiny bits of evidence as these that catch criminals, and give forensic investigators more than enough reason to spend their days "splitting hairs."

6

BOMBS

As Roger E. Moore went outside to get his newspaper on a crisp Arkansas morning on November 5, 1994, a man wearing army fatigues and a black ski mask darted in front of him and pointed a shotgun at Moore's stomach. The gunman tied Moore up and blindfolded him. After ransacking his home, he stole sixty-six rifles and eight pistols, some gold coins and silver bars, and about $8,500 in cash, then sped away in Moore's car.[1]

For the robber, this theft was the first act on the road to the bloodiest terrorist crime ever committed in America. The final act would be seared in the memories of people throughout the world—the explosion of a two-ton, homemade bomb that ripped open the Alfred P. Murrah Federal Building at 9:02 A.M. on April 19, 1995. The bomb, planted in a Ryder rental truck parked outside the building, killed at least 168 people, including 19 children who were in the building's day care center.

Charged in the bombing were Timothy McVeigh, Terry

Nichols, and Michael J. Fortier, former army buddies at Fort Riley, Kansas. Fortier admitted he drove McVeigh to Oklahoma City on December 16, 1994, to case the federal building. In return for giving evidence against McVeigh and Nichols, prosecutors allowed Fortier to plead guilty to the lesser counts of transporting stolen arms and perjury. In February 1996, Judge Richard P. Matsch of federal district court ordered the trial moved to Denver, Colorado, to insure an impartial jury, as the defense claimed McVeigh and Nichols could not get a fair trial in Oklahoma, where the defense believed public sentiment was already biased against the suspects.

A TANGLED WEB OF CLUES

Roger Moore claimed a man named McVeigh from New York was behind the robbery, but was not the robber. Moore had met McVeigh at a gun show and occasionally let him stay at his house. Moore said the robber was much shorter and stockier than McVeigh, who is six feet two inches tall and weighs 160 pounds. The mystery of the robber's identity added weight to the FBI's belief that more people than McVeigh, Fortier, and Nichols were involved in the bombing.

On May 30, a gruesome clue was found in the rubble—a human left leg clad in a size seven and a half black combat boot with an olive blousing strap, an elastic band used to tuck trousers over the top of a boot. The medical examiner's report first stated the leg was from a light-skinned, dark-haired man. Stephen Jones, a lawyer for Timothy McVeigh, speculated the leg belonged to the real bomber. Then, on August 30, results from new DNA tests and footprints indicated the leg belonged to an African-American victim, Lakesha Levy, age twenty-one, who was in the air force. This new information meant Ms. Levy might have been buried with someone else's leg. However, because eight victims were buried without their left legs, the new information also meant the leg might belong to one of them. In February 1996, permission was given to exhume Ms. Levy's body, buried in New Orleans, Louisiana. The left leg buried in her coffin was sent to the FBI laboratory for further DNA tests to try to determine for sure whose body that leg came from.[2]

The FBI believed McVeigh and Nichols were members of an organized extremist group that gave them financial support. McVeigh was known to have made a telephone call two weeks before the blast to Elohim City, the compound of an extremist Christian sect on the Arkansas-Oklahoma border. Investigators believed McVeigh's call was an appeal for help with the bombing. The phone call was traced back to a private residence in Kingman, Arizona, thought to be Fortier's trailer home.

THE BOMBERS' MOTIVATION

The three indicted men shared a hatred for the federal government. McVeigh's hatred was focused on the 1993 Bureau of Alcohol, Tobacco and Firearms (ATF) raid on the Branch Davidian compound near Waco, Texas, which ended in a fire that killed eighty members of the cult. The date of that raid was also April 19. The FBI speculated that the Oklahoma explosion was meant as revenge for the Branch Davidians. One possible explanation for choosing the federal building as a target was that Bob Ricks, the FBI agent who gave daily televised briefings during the fifty-one-day Waco siege, was at the time of the bombing in charge of the FBI's Oklahoma City office.

THE ROAD TO TERROR

The FBI tracked events leading to the Oklahoma bombing as beginning around October 1, when McVeigh and Nichols stole two hundred sticks of dynamite and several hundred blasting caps from a storage locker in Marion County, Kansas. On September 30 and October 18, in McPherson, Kansas, using the name Mike Havens, they bought four thousand pounds of ammonium nitrate fertilizer in fifty-pound bags. And on November 5, the unknown masked man robbed Roger Moore, probably to pay for explosive supplies. Enter Michael Fortier. According to the indictment, on December 16, McVeigh drove with Fortier to Kansas to get the firearms stolen in the Arkansas robbery. On the way, they cased the Murrah Federal Building.

In April, McVeigh rented the Ryder truck in which he planted the bomb, and bought a 1977 yellow Mercury Marquis to use as his getaway car. He switched the license plate on the Mercury, and perhaps he did not screw the new plate on tight enough, for it fell off as he was speeding away from the bombing. Charles J. Hanger, an Oklahoma Highway Patrol officer, stopped McVeigh for driving without a license plate in Perry, Oklahoma, at 10:20 A.M., just short of eighty minutes after the bomb went off. McVeigh got out of the car, and Hanger noticed a bulge in his jacket, under his left arm. McVeigh opened his jacket, and hanging in a shoulder holster was a .45-caliber Glock military assault pistol with a Black Talon impact-expanding bullet in the chamber. Hanger confiscated the gun, along with a fixed-blade knife that McVeigh carried in a sheath on his belt.

McVeigh told Hanger he was in the process of moving to Arkansas. He had taken one load of his belongings there and was now returning for another load. Hanger took McVeigh to jail, where he was charged with carrying a concealed weapon, transporting a loaded firearm in a vehicle, failing to display a license plate, and having no insurance.

At that point, no one thought McVeigh was involved in the bombing. The next day, Thursday, his bail hearing was delayed for a day when the judge in charge of his case became tied up in a complicated divorce case. On Friday morning, McVeigh was brought down for his court hearing about 10:30 A.M. While he was waiting for his court appearance, Sheriff Jerry Cook received a call from an ATF agent inquiring whether they had McVeigh in custody, explaining that he was thought to be connected to the bombing. Deputies immediately whisked McVeigh back to jail and set up a special security system around his cell. The FBI arrived around noon and placed him under arrest for the bombing of the federal building. If it had not been for the delay in McVeigh's bail hearing, he might have been set free on bail before the ATF agents caught up with him. And once out on bail, he could have gone into hiding and never been caught.

FERTILIZER CAN BE DEADLY

When spread on a field of corn, ammonium nitrate, the white crystalline chemical compound found in fertilizer, becomes an enrichment to soil. But mix it with fuel oil, and it becomes a lethal explosive. The United States makes eight million tons of ammonium nitrate each year, which can be bought by anyone at gardening centers, supply warehouses, and construction sites.

Some 95 percent of all commercial explosive work in the United States uses ammonium nitrate and fuel oil in specially prepared mixtures called ANFO. You can light a match to ANFO, jump on it, even shoot a bullet at it, but it is not likely to blow up, according to Jeffrey Dean, executive director of the International Society of Explosives Engineers in Cleveland, Ohio.[3] To explode ANFO, demolition workers must use both a detonator containing a small amount of a highly explosive material, and a booster charge to create a shock wave to set off the chemical. A special type of detonator called a blasting cap is most frequently used, and its sale is tightly controlled. Investigators believe the Oklahoma City bomb was set off by nonelectric igniters and blasting caps used in military demolition work. The use of commercial ANFO is strictly monitored. Anyone wanting to buy it must have a federal permit issued by the ATF. They must also have a permit from the Department of Transportation to move ANFO.

But someone with a knowledge of chemistry could make the explosive by using ammonium nitrate fertilizer and diesel fuel.

Commercially bought fertilizer must be treated to get rid of impurities before it can be converted into an explosive substance. Information on how to purify fertilizer is available in books and even on the Internet. Yet even with all this information at their fingertips, amateur bombers can easily make a mistake and blow themselves up.

In the early part of the twentieth century, bombings were a rare crime. A few sticks of dynamite were used by political anarchists in the 1920s to fight for the rights of workers' unions. In the 1930s, gangsters used stench, or stink bombs to damage restaurants and movie theaters whose owners refused to sell their businesses to the mob. Most citizens were not affected by bombs at all.

Then on November 1, 1955, United Airlines Flight 629 exploded in midair after taking off from Denver, and a new kind of bomber appeared on the scene—one who would plant bombs in public places in order to kill one person. In the 1960s, bombs were used by people fighting integration in the South. In one horrendous crime, six little girls were killed when a church attended by African-Americans was bombed in Birmingham, Alabama. It was this bombing that spurred the creation of an Explosives Unit at the FBI Crime Lab.

BOMB SIGNATURES

Because there are an endless number of ways to make a bomb, bombers develop their own individual techniques. These techniques become their signatures. Even if given exactly the same components, two bombers will not make the same bomb.

Bombs, more than any other type of weapon, make people easy targets. Unlike guns, bombs do not have to be aimed in order to inflict their damage. Unlike poison, bombs do not have to be administered to the victims. In fact, bombers do not have to be anywhere near their victims to set off the explosive. And bombs kill randomly, making them the prime weapon used by terrorists.

Parts of a Bomb

There are three parts to every bomb: the power source, such as a flashlight battery or an electrical wire; the trigger, such as heat, shock, or friction; and the explosive substance, such as dynamite or nitroglycerin. The power source causes the trigger to start a reaction in the explosive substance. When this happens, the substance breaks apart its chemical bonds, releasing gases that take up a greater space than the original solid or liquid. The release of gases starts a tremendous shock wave that rips apart anything that confines it, such as the box or suitcase the bomb is planted in. This ripping apart creates a vacuum that draws the gases back toward the bomb site. For this reason, there may be more shattered glass on the inside of a bomb-site building than on the outside.[4]

The World Trade Center Bombing

What happened when New York City's World Trade Center was bombed just after 12:00 noon on February 26, 1993, is an example of the powerful pressure wave of a bomb. Seconds before the bomb went off, a Center employee's husband dropped her and their infant son off outside the building. When the bomb exploded, the pressure wave it created ripped out a three-foot section of guardrail located in the garage's basement level, crushed it into a twenty-five-pound metal ball, and flung it three hundred yards up the five-level parking ramp onto the street. Then this metal ball shot through the rear window of the husband's car on the driver's side, hitting the infant seat, where their baby sat only minutes before. Still going strong, the "bomb-bullet" veered off between the bucket seats and embedded itself in the dashboard. If it had not hit the infant's seat first, the ball would have knocked the husband's head off.

TRACKING THE BOMB

Each bombing investigation involves four steps. First, identify the bomb's components and associate them with the person who bought them or made them. Second, compare the bomb's construction with other bombs that have been linked to specific people. Explosives experts do this by blowing up different things to see what kind of damage a particular type of bomb causes. As FBI explosive expert Fred Smith says, "If you want to know what certain explosive charges will do to an automobile, you blow up a lot of automobiles."[5]

The third step in explosives investigations is to identify evidence found at the scene that is not part of the bomb—the car used to transport it, a fingerprint on the wrapping paper—and trace that evidence to the bomber. And fourth, find the motive for the bombing. It is often the motive that leads directly to the bomber.

FINDING THE BOMB

Agents began by looking for residues that would tell what type of explosive was used in the World Trade Center bombing. None were found. But a high percentage of nitric acid and urea were found. It turned out the explosive was a mixture called urea nitrate, a homemade explosive. In more than seventy thousand bombings since 1971, the only other time agents had seen it used was in Rockville, Maryland, in 1988, when four college students were making a pipe bomb and it exploded, killing all four.[6] What made discovering the type of explosive difficult was that an explosion breaks down urea nitrate into urea and nitric acid, two chemicals that are common in nature, and thus could have come from anywhere. Therefore, finding urea and nitric acid in the debris did not necessarily mean they were part of the explosive used in the World Trade Center bombing. But by looking at the way the damage was spread out, agents did know the force from the bomb had not been directed right, left, up, or down, meaning the explosive was probably laid in a large container, such as a plastic trash can.

Different explosives detonate at different speeds and cause different types of damage, depending on those speeds. The kind of damage done to the World Trade Center indicated that the speed of this bomb was between 14,000 to 15,000 feet per second. In order to attain this speed, the bomb had to be fertilizer-based, and weigh about 1,200 pounds. Anything faster or slower would cause a different type of damage. Now the question was how did the bomber get 1,200 pounds of explosive into the building? A car would be too small, and the building's garage door was not high enough to permit a large truck to enter. So investigators guessed the bomb was carried in a one-ton van or truck. That was an important clue. For now investigators knew what type of vehicle to look for. And sure enough, a piece of rear frame rail from a van was found that had either been carrying the bomb or was close to the blast.

Every vehicle manufactured in the United States has a vehicle identification number (VIN), an identification number the manufacturer stamps on the dashboard. But vehicles also have a confidential ID number, called a CVIN. It is the same number as the VIN, but is stamped in three other places, and those places differ from vehicle to vehicle. Therefore, if you steal a car, you would have to dismantle it to find those CVIN numbers so you could get rid of them. By sheer luck, the van piece found at the site of the World Trade Center bombing had a visible CVIN. The number was put into the National Criminal Intelligence Center computer, and the vehicle was identified as a Ford Econoline van owned by the Ryder rental agency. Investigators determined it had been rented in Jersey City, New Jersey, by Mohammed Salameh and had been reported stolen the day before the bombing. Incredibly, Salameh had contacted

Ryder to get his $400 deposit back. FBI agents believe he risked capture by contacting the rental agency because the bombers thought the van would be totally destroyed in the explosion. Salameh was arrested when he showed up at the rental office for his deposit.

Now agents had to prove Salameh was responsible for the Trade Center bomb. His personal records led agents to Nidal Ayyad and Mahmud Abouhalima, who had helped Salameh make the bomb. After reading about the arrest in the newspaper, the owner of a Jersey City storage facility contacted the Newark FBI to say the day before the bombing he saw four men loading a Ryder van. He checked their storage space and found some chemicals inside. Investigators went to the site and found 300 pounds of urea, 250 pounds of sulfuric acid, a dozen bottles of nitric acid, two 50-foot lengths of hobby fuse, a pump, a light blue, 32-gallon Rubbermaid trash can, and six 2-quart bottles of homemade nitroglycerin—everything needed to make a 300-pound bomb. Also found were pamphlets and a videotape describing how to make urea nitrate, which were traced to a fourth suspect, Ahmad Ajaj.

The hobby fuse clued investigators that the bomb's detonation system was a nonelectric burning type, meaning the bombers lit it and ran away fast. Records from Ayyad's house showed he purchased three tanks of hydrogen from AGL Welding Supply in Clifton, New Jersey. In an explosion, hydrogen acts as an accelerant. The remains of three hydrogen tanks with "AGL Welding" stamped on their sides were found in the World Trade Center debris. A Materials Analysis Unit proved that specks of blue plastic found on the remains of a rear post from the van were consistent with the blue trash can found in the storage area. After the bombing, the *New York Times* received a letter from a group calling itself the Fifth Liberation Brigade, claiming responsibility for the bombing. Ayyad's computer was removed from his desk at the Allied-Signal Company, where he worked. In files retrieved from the computer's hard drive, files that Ayyad had tried to delete, the exact words from that letter were found, indicating the letter had been written on Ayyad's computer. The DNA Unit developed a DNA profile from the saliva used to seal the envelope. It matched a saliva sample taken from Ayyad. The men were each sentenced to 240 years in prison.[7]

PAN AM FLIGHT 103: THE ANATOMY OF A BOMBING

The investigation of the bombing of Pan Am Flight 103 over Lockerbie, Scotland, on December 21, 1988, is thought by many forensic investigators to be both the most complex and most successful bomb scene search in history. The most important piece of debris was half the size of a thumbnail, found the first day of the search. It later proved to have come from the skid rail of the luggage container in which the bomb had been planted. This meant the bomb had been in the baggage compartment, rather than in the passenger cabin.

Residues on the rail were identified as PETN and RDX. The only explosive known to contain these two residues is Semtex, a favorite of terrorists. This meant the bombing was probably a terrorist act rather than murder for revenge or money. On Christmas morning, the other piece of the skid rail was found. The odds against finding this other half cannot even be figured. Now the question was which luggage container the bomb had been in. Knowing that could tell exactly where the bomb had been put aboard the airplane.

FINDING WHERE THE BOMB WAS PLANTED

Like putting Humpty Dumpty back together again, FBI agents began putting the airplane back together in a hangar at Farnborough Royal Air Force Base, south of London. A wire frame was set up, and as each piece arrived from Lockerbie it was hung where it belonged. Investigators noticed about seven hundred inches back from the baggage compartment was a big hole. The cargo manifest showed a container labeled AVE4041PA had been exactly where the hole was.

The broken baggage containers were also reconstructed. The sides of these containers had ID numbers stenciled on them, so it was easy to spot #AVE4041PA. Like the other containers, this one had a hole in the base due to the force of the explosion. But the sides of this hole were bent down at almost a ninety-degree angle. Agents knew this was the container the bomb had been planted in, and where it was located on the airplane.

HOW THE BOMB WAS MADE

Now investigators had to find how the bomb was made and what it was placed in before ending up in the baggage compartment. Also in the baggage container was found a piece of plastic circuit board equipped with European frequencies that had come from a long and narrow cassette radio. Investigators took the circuit board recovered from the crash site to Toshiba, and the company confirmed the board had come from one of their radios. This was a vital clue, as it meant the bomb had been built inside a Toshiba radio.

Weeks earlier, the then West German government had raided an apartment used by a terrorist organization known as the Popular Front for the Liberation of Palestine-General Command. In the trunk of the leader's car, they found a quantity of Semtex explosive and a Toshiba radio with an altimeter fuse. The only place an altimeter fuse is any good on is an airplane. It meant the bomb had been set to explode when the plane reached a certain altitude. Finding both Semtex explosive and a Toshiba radio in the terrorist leader's car trunk—the same explosive and type of radio used in building the bomb on Pan Am Flight 103—while not 100 percent proof that a member, or members, of the Popular Front organization had planted the bomb, did link the terrorist group to the bombing. From baggage fragments, investigators even knew what type of suitcase the bomb had been put in. The cargo manifest was checked to learn when that suitcase had been put on the plane. Records showed the suitcase had originally been aboard Air Malta Flight KM-190, which had connected with Pan Am 103 in Frankfurt, Germany.

BACK TO THE CIRCUIT BOARD

Early in 1990, more than a year after the crash, an English detective examining clothing that had been in the suitcase with the bomb found a tiny piece of green circuit board embedded in a shirt. It did not come from the Toshiba radio. Investigators speculated it came from the timing mechanism used to detonate the bomb. From millions of pieces of airplane wreckage, a detective had literally found the "needle in the haystack," a real piece of the actual bomb.

Now agents tried to find where the timing mechanism circuit board had come from. It was made of fiberglass, with an unusual curved notch in it. An FBI agent in Washington remembered similar timers used in two bombs recovered from the African nation of Togo in a 1986 failed coup. The agent found the two bombs in the agency's evidence storage area. When the backs of the timers were opened, agents hit pay dirt. The circuit board was just like the piece of circuit board found embedded in the shirt.

Parts of the African timer were examined under a microscope, and the circuit patterns matched the piece of circuit from the Pan Am bombing. Some printing had been scratched out on one of the circuits. Infrared photography brought up the letter *m* and either a 5 or a *B*. A Swiss company, Meister et Bollier, that makes high-quality timers for many legitimate purposes had just those initials. The company's managing director identified the piece of circuit board. Between 1985 and 1986, twenty of these timers had been delivered to a Libyan official, and several more were sold to what was then East Germany. The SATs, East Germany's secret police, had extensive contacts with Syria-based Palestinian terrorists.

Further, some clothing recovered from the suitcase in which the bomb was planted came from a Mary's House clothing store in Sliema, Malta, located near the Libyan embassy on Malta. The owner of the store identified photographs of a known Libyan intelligence agent named Abdel Basset Ali Al-Magrahi as the person who had bought the clothing found in the suitcase. Agents on Malta learned Basset had arrived on the island on December 20, 1988, a day before the bombing. He was met by a second Libyan intelligence agent, Lamen Khalifa Fhimah, who had been the station manager on Malta for Libyan Arab Airlines. That position gave him access to airline baggage without having to go through normal security checks.

So from two pieces of plastic, both shorter than two inches, buried in millions of fragments of charred debris, two killers were found. Basset and Fhimah were indicted in November 1991. Incredibly, however, they have never been arrested. Libyan ruler Mu'ammar Gadhafi refuses to extradite the killers to the West for trial.[8]

THE UNABOMBER

On April 24, 1995, Gilbert Murray, president of the California Forestry Association in Sacramento, California, received a package in the mail. As he started to unwrap it, the package blew up in his hands, killing him instantly. Association workers swarmed into the streets in fear and panic. They still had the Oklahoma bombing from a week earlier on their minds. But unlike the crude bomb that destroyed the Murrah Federal Building, this bomb was carefully put together. And unlike the Oklahoma bombing, investigators immediately knew who the bomber was.

For he had left his usual signature. This killer had been exploding package bombs for the past seventeen years, and the FBI had given him the code name: "Unabomber."

The Unabomber was given that nickname because his original targets were university faculty and airlines (thus the *un* and the *a* placed before the word *bomber*). His first bomb exploded in 1978 in the technical building of Northwestern University, in Evanston, Illinois, injuring one person.

Since then, a mail bomb attributed to the Unabomber exploded every year, except the years between 1982 through 1985. FBI investigators believed the three-year gap in bombings may have been due to his being either in prison or in an institution during that time. In all, the Unabomber killed three people and injured at least twenty-three, in cities from Connecticut to California. To help catch him, the FBI set up a San Francisco-based Unabomber Task Force in 1993, run jointly by the FBI, the ATF, and the post office.

BARGAINING WITH A BOMBER

Until the 1995 bombing, the FBI did not know for certain the motive behind the bomber's killing spree. Because the targets had been scientists or people involved with technology, investigators suspected the bomber had a grudge against technology. Then, in April of that year, the Unabomber sent letters to the *New York Times*, the *Washington Post*, a national magazine, and to David Gelernter, a Yale computer scientist who lost part of a hand, the vision in one eye, and the hearing in one ear in the Unabomber's 1993 blast.

"Through our bombings," the letter said, "we hope to promote social instability in industrial society, propagate anti-industrial ideas and give encouragement to those who hate the industrial system."[9] The letters confirmed investigators' theories that the Unabomber's motivation was a hatred toward industry and technology. Despite the word *we* used in the letter, and his claim to be part of an anarchist group called the Freedom Club, most investigators believed the Unabomber was acting alone.

Along with the letters, the Unabomber sent a thirty-five-hundred-word manuscript entitled *Industrial Society and Its Future*, stating the alleged group's belief that industrial and technological progress have robbed humans of their self-esteem, and the only alternative is a revolution against technology. He gave the newspapers three months to publish the tract, or he would bomb again. That bargain created an ethical journalistic dilemma. Should editors publish the material and possibly save lives, or refuse to surrender to the demands of a terrorist? After deliberating practically up to the Unabomber's deadline, on September 19, 1995, editors at the *New York Times* and the *Washington Post* complied with a request from Attorney General Janet Reno and FBI Director Louis J. Freeh to publish the manuscript. The editors split the cost of publishing, but printed the tract in the *Post*, which had the mechanical ability to distribute a separate section in all copies of its daily paper. FBI Agent Jim R. Freeman, head of the Unabomber Task Force, said the publication of the tract could help crack the case, because someone reading it might recognize the writing as that of someone they know and notify the FBI.

OTHER CLUES

A promising clue to the Unabomber's identity was revealed on February 20, 1987, when a witness spotted someone leaving what proved to be a bomb outside a computer store in Salt Lake City, Utah. The witness gave a physical description to the FBI, which was the basis for the composite sketch in FBI "wanted" posters. He was believed to be 5 feet 10 inches to 6 feet tall, weigh about 165 pounds, have reddish blond hair, a thin mustache, a ruddy complexion, and wear glasses. In addition, the fact that the Unabomber had placed bombs in Sacramento and Berkeley, and used a Sacramento State University faculty member's name on a 1993 bomb's return address, made investigators suspect the Unabomber was based in northern California.

THE UNABOMBER'S SIGNATURE Fragments found from the Unabomber's bombs told investigators he made them from scrap material, with many parts carved from wood. In addition, he made some of his own metal parts, including filing down wires to make nails. He used several different types of powder in each bomb, so he did not have to get his explosives from one source, which could call attention to himself. Each bomb was generally placed in a homemade wooden box before being mailed or delivered. He scratched the initials "FC" on the bombs, standing for his alleged "Freedom Club."

PSYCHOLOGICAL PROFILE FBI forensic psychologists compiled a mental and emotional profile of the Unabomber. He was thought to be a white male, in his thirties or forties, with low self-esteem, but with at least a high school education. His attention to detail in his bombs pointed to a person with an obsessive personality, who was meticulously organized and liked to make lists. In addition, he probably was a man with a "back-to-the-woods" philosophy of life, which was thought to explain his obsession with using wood parts in his bombs, and his April, 1995, targeting of the California Forestry Association, which represents logging companies. Treasury Department officials offered a one million dollar reward for information leading to the arrest and conviction of the Unabomber.[10]

THE END OF THE HUNT

On April 3, 1996, the search for America's most-wanted killer came to an end. The FBI hypothesized that if the Unabomber's manifesto were printed, someone might recognize the philosophy or writing style as coming from a person they knew and notify authorities. They never imagined who that someone would be. The informant was the killer's own brother. When

David Kaczynski, a social worker in New York, was helping his mother move out of her house in Lombard, Illinois, in 1995, he stumbled across some copies of letters his brother had written to newspapers years earlier. The letters' contents were almost exactly like the manifesto's theme protesting against industrial society. Hoping to prevent any more bombing deaths, David notified the FBI of his suspicions in February 1996.[11]

Investigators agreed there were striking similarities between the letters and the manifesto. Both contained the word "pre-industrial" written with a hyphen, but the compound word "smallscale" written without one. Certain words were always misspelled, such as "analyse," rather than "analyze," "wilfully," instead of "willfully," and "instalment," instead of "installment." Both the manifesto and a letter to David's mother reversed a cliché, writing that "you can't eat your cake and have it too."[12]

Who was the Unabomber? He was Theodore (Ted) John Kaczynski, a 54-year-old recluse living in the mountains outside of Lincoln, Montana, in a 10-by-12-foot handmade plywood shack with no electricity or running water. Ironically, in order to enter the cabin safely, FBI agents used the same high-tech devices the Unabomber preached against. First, agents bombarded the cabin with electromagnetic energy, similar to an X ray, to create a three-dimensional picture of the room, allowing agents to "see" if there were any electronically operated booby traps inside.

When both a partially completed and a completed pipe bomb were pictured in the X ray, agents sent in a remote-controlled robot to retrieve the bombs. Once outside, the bombs were defused, then sent to the FBI lab to be analyzed. Agents found the bombs to be similar to an explosive device used in one of the Unabomber's attacks.[13]

Agents found books on bombmaking, notebooks containing data on chemical compounds that create explosive charges, test results on bombs, C-cell batteries, electrical wire, galvanized metal, powder to fuel pipe bombs, and wood-carving instruments with marks that were later found to match marks left on fragments recovered from the bombs in Kaczynski's cabin.[14]

Investigators also made a connection between the dates Ted received checks from his mother and brother and the dates of the bombings. On December 5, 1985, Ted received a $600 check, and on December 11, Hugh Scrutton of Sacramento was killed by a mail bomb. Ted got a $1,000 check in November 1994, a month before Thomas Mosser of New Jersey was killed by a bomb. He got a $2,000 check in February 1995, two months before California Forestry Association President Gilbert Murray was killed opening a mail bomb. Investigators believe the checks gave Ted the money to make and mail the bombs.[15]

Some of the most damaging pieces of evidence against Kaczynski were a hooded sweatshirt and aviator sunglasses found in his cabin that resemble those worn by the Unabomber when he was spotted placing a bomb in Utah; positive tests matching fingerprints inside the cabin to fingerprints found on bomb fragments and letters sent by the Unabomber; and DNA from his saliva taken from a stamp and envelope he sent his brother, which matched DNA from saliva on stamps licked by the Unabomber to mail copies of his manifesto to the newspapers. But the most significant discovery of all was what appears to be the original manifesto. It matches carbon copies sent by the Unabomber to newspapers. In addition, one of the three typewriters found in the cabin appears to match not only the one that produced the manifesto, but also typed material recovered from bomb scenes and a letter sent to the *New York Times* demanding the manifesto be published.[16]

What makes up the man accused of being the Unabomber? Ted Kaczynski was born in Chicago, in 1942, the son of a Polish sausagemaker. He was a smart student, skipping his junior year of high school. Just as the FBI profile speculated, he was a loner, never making friends. He did have one hobby: putting things together to create explosions. A classmate, Dale Eickelman, now a professor at Dartmouth College, remembers detonating explosives in garbage cans with Ted, using ingredients they scrounged up around the house. Kaczynski's mother, Wanda, wrote a letter to Harvard University about her son, saying "Much of his time is spent . . . contriving gadgets made of wood, string, wire, tape, etc. His table and desk are a mess of test tubes, chemicals, batteries, ground coal, etc."[17]

Ted went to Harvard at age 16. Students there cannot remember ever having a conversation with him. "Ted had a special talent for avoiding relationships by moving quickly past groups of people and slamming the door behind him," says Patrick McIntosh, one of Ted's dorm mates.[18] Kaczynski graduated from Harvard at age 20, then received a master's degree and a doctorate in math from the University of Michigan. He then taught math at the University of California, Berkeley, resigning after two years. In 1971, he built his cabin in Montana and lived on whatever he could grow or kill, sometimes doing odd jobs to make money for supplies.

On June 21, 1996, Ted Kaczynski was formally charged with being the Unabomber, responsible for four bombings, and illegally transporting and mailing bombs. The charges carry penalties of life in prison or death. He was flown to Sacramento, California, for trial, which is expected to begin sometime in 1997. Maybe then the world will find out more about the bomber who eluded capture for seventeen years.[19]

In bombings, forensic scientists look at fragments of the bomb and debris from the explosion to lead them to the killer. In murders not caused by bombs, investigators often find the killer by looking at a more gruesome clue—the body of the victim itself.

7

CORPSES AND SKELETONS
CLUES THE DEAD LEAVE

In August 1974, Malcolm and Eleanor Graham, a middle-aged couple, disappeared while sailing around the world on their yacht. A younger couple, Buck Walker and Jennifer Jenkins, were found sailing their boat. They were convicted of theft. But for seven years, there was no trace of the Grahams. Then a trunk washed up on a deserted beach on Palmyra Island, one thousand miles south of Hawaii. Lying nearby in the sand was a scorched human skull with a gold dental crown. Dental X rays confirmed the crown came from Eleanor Graham. Circumstantial evidence linked the trunk to the Grahams. A skeleton and human hairs were found inside the trunk, but there was no way of proving when the remains got there. The trunk was sent to the FBI forensic laboratory for further examination. One of the biologists found white residue caked on the inside surface of the trunk. Microscopic examination of the residue showed it was adipocere, a product formed when fatty tissue decomposes under anaerobic conditions, meaning without oxygen. The trunk had been under the sea, a place without oxygen. The presence of adipocere proved something that was once alive had been in the trunk. And examination of the skeletal bones concluded they came from a Caucasian woman.

But there was still no proof of how long the trunk had been in the sea—until a special "detective" made its presence known. The "detective" was a worm. In further examining the trunk, biologists found the shell of a worm on the bottom of the trunk. This worm grows only on the underside of a submerged object, and lives six months before shedding its shell. This proved the trunk had been in the ocean for at least six months, maybe for as long as seven years. Buck Walker was convicted of murdering Eleanor Graham.[1] The remains of Malcolm Graham have never been found.

SKELETONS

The dead tell no tales, goes an old saying. But as the above case shows, remains of murder victims hold clues to their killers. In some cases, a death has occurred so long ago that only the skeleton remains. Forensic anthropologists, scientists who study the bone structure of ancient and modern humans, can determine an amazing amount of information by studying a skeleton.

WHOSE SKELETON IS IT ?

The FBI's forensic lab often works with the Smithsonian Institution in Washington, D.C., in documenting anthropological cases. "The first thing we do," says Douglas Owsley, Ph.D., a forensic anthropologist with the Smithsonian Institution, "is figure out whether the bones are even human."[2] Twenty-five percent of the time, the bones are from animals. If the bones are human, the shape and size of the pelvic bones reveal the body's sex, the skull its race, the development of joints its age, and the length of leg bones its height. The size of ridges on the bones where muscles attach indicates the strength and size of the muscle development of the person. Larger ridges on the left arm would person was left-handed. A broken hyoid bone, whi the larynx (Adam's apple), may indicate the victim wa Holes in the ribs or skull may mark the penetration c

In addition, a person's lifestyle can be determined by the condition of his or her teeth. Certain kinds of grooves worn in the teeth most likely mean the person smoked a pipe. Dr. Owsley once examined a skeleton found near colonial Jamestown. "I realized the woman was a seamstress by scanning her teeth with an electron microscope. I could see the distinctive notches made by a lifetime of holding pins in her mouth."[3]

Babies have soft spots on their heads because the bones that make up the skull have not yet fused. Total fusion of skull bones occurs around age twenty-five. By examining the skull, anthropologists can approximate the age of the victim.

CALL IN THE FORENSIC SCULPTOR

When a skull is found, it is possible to reconstruct a three-dimensional sculpture of the corpse's face. Using known values of the thickness of flesh over specific parts of the skull, a forensic sculptor can produce an amazingly accurate representation of what a person may have looked like, based only on their skull.

In early 1989, the TV program *America's Most Wanted* used a sculpture to show an age-adjusted bust of John List, of Westfield, New Jersey. The bust, made of clay, was sculpted by Frank Bender, a forensic sculptor. He looked at old photographs of List, provided by the police, to guide him, while also taking into account how eighteen years of aging would affect List's face. List had been wanted by the police since 1971 for shooting his wife, mother, and three children. After the broadcast, three hundred calls came in, reporting sightings of List. One of the calls led FBI agents to the home of Mr. and Mrs. Robert Clark in Richmond, Virginia. A frightened Mrs. Clark was stunned by the resemblance of her husband to both the old pictures of John List shown to her by the FBI agents, and the reconstructed just. When agents questioned Mr. Clark, they noticed a scar behind his ear, indicating he had undergone a type of surgery known to have been performed on List. And one other thing he couldn't deny: his fingerprints matched those of John List. Robert Clark was the long-sought murderer.

TECHNOLOGY COMES INTO THE PICTURE

Today's digitalized computer technology has catapulted forensic investigation into the space age. Like sculptures, computer software can reconstruct a victim's face when only the skull is found.

But computers can also create an age-adjusted picture of a face, showing what a person who disappeared several years ago probably looks like today. Working from the last known photo of a person, a computer technician can age that photo by any number of years. This technology is especially valuable in locating missing children. Many kidnapped children have been found after someone saw their age-adjusted faces on posters or postcards.

SKELETONS FROM THE PAST

"The evil men do lives after them; the good is oft interred with their bones," wrote Shakespeare. For murder victims, what is interred with their bones are clues to their killers. To help solve murders committed many years ago, forensic anthropologists like Dr. James Starrs, professor of forensic sciences at George Washington University in Washington, D.C., use modern forensic techniques on skeletal remains to get new clues.

On the night of September 8, 1935, Dr. Carl Austin Weiss, twenty-nine, allegedly jumped from behind a marble pillar in the state capitol building in Baton Rouge, Louisiana, and shot the controversial former governor, Huey P. Long. Long's bodyguards then shot and killed Weiss. Some people believe the murderers were Long's bodyguards, who intentionally shot Weiss to make it look like an assassination.

Exhuming the body of Huey Long is impossible, as he is buried under a sixty-ton concrete shrine in Baton Rouge. So on October 20, 1991, Professor Starrs and his team exhumed the body of Carl Weiss. He took the remains to the Smithsonian Institution for examination. "The first thing you try to do is determine which direction the bullets came from," says Starrs.[4] Eleven bullets had been fired into Weiss's back. Yet at the inquest, the bodyguards testified they had not seen Weiss shot in the back.

Perhaps the clearest evidence that the bodyguards were lying came from fibers found in bullets taken from Carl Weiss's head. These fibers indicated the bullets struck something before hitting Weiss. A photograph of Weiss lying dead in the capitol building shows a bullet hole in his left wrist, indicating he threw up his arm to protect himself, and the bullet struck the shirt cuff covering his wrist before entering his skull. The bodyguards were asked what Weiss was doing when they opened fire. All said he was crouched down as if he were about to shoot. But the fibers on the bullets say otherwise. Starrs never did prove who actually fired the shot that killed Long. But his findings cast enough doubt on who the real murderer was to prevent historians from conclusively blaming Carl Weiss.

THE CASE OF LIZZIE BORDEN

In the future, Starrs hopes to shed new light on one of the most famous murder cases in American history. Did Lizzie Borden, as the old rhyme says, "give her mother 40 whacks, and when the job was nicely done, give her father 41"?

In August 1892, Abby and Andrew Borden were found hacked to death in their home in Fall River, Massachusetts. In America's first tabloid murder trial, twenty-three-year-old Lizzie Borden was acquitted of the murders. But some people still believe she was guilty. The mystery lingers, as there were no witnesses to the killings, the bodies were found in different rooms, and the deaths occurred more than an hour apart.

The hatchet on exhibit at the Fall River Historical Society is thought by some not to be the murder weapon at all, even though it is the one presented at the trial. Starrs wants to examine the hatchet with scientific methods nonexistent a century ago. And if permission is granted to exhume the Borden's bodies, the DNA content in their bone marrow can be compared with the DNA of any blood flecks remaining on the hatchet. In addition, hatchet blows to the victims' heads can be compared with a detailed picture of the metal blade created with the aid of an electron microscope. As the hatchet passes through bone, it may leave a mark characteristic only to that hatchet. Either way, Starrs could prove conclusively whether or not the hatchet was the murder weapon.

THE MISSING HEADS The problem is that no one is sure the heads of the murdered Bordens are buried with their bodies. Prior to their burial, Harvard University requested the heads be removed and sent to their lab for study. There is no record whether they were ever returned to Fall River. So Starrs must prove the skulls are there in order to convince a Massachusetts judge that useful information will be gained by granting an exhumation order. Professor Starrs is currently sweeping the cemetery where the Bordens are buried with a radar device, hoping the instrument will penetrate the ground and "see" a box that some people say contains the skulls and was buried three feet from the bodies. If he finds the missing heads, we may finally know whether the hatchet on exhibit is the true murder weapon.

TIME OF DEATH

Once the identity of a body is known, the next step is finding out when the murder or suicide occurred. Then detectives can ask suspects the familiar question, "Where were you on the night of . . . ?" Until recently, medical examiners could estimate time of death only for the first forty-eight hours after the victim died. Today, however, when a body has been dead for much longer, another scientific team member picks up the ball—the forensic entomologist. These scientists study a particularly gruesome type of evidence on a corpse—bugs!

INSECT SLEUTHS

Years ago, medical examiners washed down corpses in their autopsy rooms, and a wealth of evidence went down the drain. Today they know that within hours of death, as a body starts to decompose, it attracts insects that feed on the corpse and lay eggs. Different stages of decomposition attract different species of insects, all within an established time frame. The insect species and the stage of the life cycle the insect is in on a body help entomologists narrow down the time a person died. In fact, insects on a dead body are as good a tool for establishing time of death as a broken watch found on the victim's wrist, with the hands stopped at an exact hour and minute.

FLIES   Flies, especially blowflies, not only attack your picnic basket, but also infest a corpse within minutes of death. This is because flies lay eggs on dying tissue. Tiny maggots, which look like wiggling grains of rice, form inside each egg. Maggots can consume 60 percent of a corpse in less than a week. During this time, they have molted twice and grown ten times their original size.

When the feeding stage is over, the maggots' skin darkens, hardens, and contracts into a barrel-shaped silica (cocoon), which takes ten hours to reach its darkest shade, a sign of the pupal stage. In a few days, an adult fly emerges from the silica. The entire cycle takes about ten days in warm weather, and twice as long in cool weather. Thus, the stage of the life cycle that blowflies are in when found on a corpse acts as a stopwatch indicating the time of death. Although the exact hour and minute of death cannot be determined, the insects found on a corpse can be used to estimate a victim's time of death to within a narrow range. In forensic terms this range is called the post-mortem interval, or the PMI.[5]

When the body of a man stabbed to death in Burlington, North Dakota, was discovered around 6:00 P.M., two eyewitnesses gave conflicting reports. One said he saw a fight between the victim and another man at 1:00 A.M. The other witness said he saw the victim alive nine hours later, at 10:00 A.M. Could they both be right? Fly eggs taken from the body were a couple of hours from hatching. From a fly colony in the forensic laboratory, entomologists collected fly eggs from the same species as found on the victim. The eggs were incubated at the same temperature as the murder scene to see how long it would take the eggs to get to the same stage as those found on the body. The eggs were found to be at least fourteen hours old. This meant they had been laid in the early morning hours of the previous day, disproving the second eyewitness's story.[6]

BLACKFLIES   Blackfly larvae have iridescent feeding fans to trap microscopic food. These fans attach to any hard surface. In April, the larvae spin silken cocoons from which adult flies emerge. When a car containing the body of a woman was found at the bottom of a river in June, her husband said he had last seen her a few weeks earlier. But the presence of blackfly larvae on the bumper of the car proved it had been in the water since April, when these larvae spin their cocoons. The husband was found guilty of murdering his wife and pushing her car into the river.[7]

BEETLES   The more time that has passed before a body's discovery, the harder it is to estimate time of death. However, forensic entomologists can calculate the time of death to within a week, even after two months have passed. In one case, the bodies of two elderly women were found years after they died in a house in Indianapolis, Indiana. Although the coroner could not tell what year the women died, he was able to say they died in October by looking at the species of beetle casings on the bodies. That particular beetle sheds its cocoon in October. When a diary was found belonging to one of the women, the last entry was dated October 5, ten years earlier.[8]

CATERPILLARS One species of caterpillar seed moth spins a silken cocoon only in May and early June. In the summer of 1980, an Illinois woman was sexually assaulted by a man wearing a ski mask. The ski mask was found in the apartment of a suspect, who claimed it had not been used since the previous winter. But seed burrs found on the mask contained mature seed moths that had just emerged from their cocoons. The seed burrs were obviously fresh. Last summer's moths would have already emerged from the burrs—proof that the suspect was lying.

HAS THE BODY BEEN MOVED?

Forensic entomologists can also tell whether a killer has moved his victim from the murder scene in order to lead police astray. One indication that a body has been moved is when the types of insects found on top of the body are different from those found underneath. And insect species on a corpse that do not belong in a certain environment, or even a certain country, are another clue that a body has been moved. If a corpse is found abandoned in a rural area, such as a woods, for example, but it has city fly larvae on it, then the murder was probably committed in the city and the body moved to the woods. It is also possible to tell if a victim was killed indoors, then moved outside, by the presence of fly larvae that do not deposit eggs outdoors.[9]

Insects Tell How the Victim Was Killed

Creepy crawlers on a corpse can also provide information as to the manner of death. Flies are normally attracted to exposed soft tissues, such as the eyes, nose, and mouth. But if a body is bleeding, flies will also lay eggs on the injury where the blood is coming from. In fact, the presence of maggots on a body may clue medical examiners in on an unseen wound.

If drugs are suspected in a death and the body is too decomposed to check for toxicological evidence, scientists can analyze the blood in insects found on the corpse for the presence of drugs. When insects feed on a corpse, they also consume any chemicals in the blood and tissues of the body. Cocaine use can be revealed, for example, by the overly rapid growth of feeding maggots.

DNA and Insects

Future advances in forensic techniques could provide such accurate means for entomologists to use insects as clues to murders that killers will literally have to fumigate the crime scene in order to erase those clues. Because mosquitoes are bloodsuckers, mosquitoes collected at crime scenes may supply forensic experts with samples of human DNA. This DNA can be compared with DNA samples taken from the suspect. A match would place that suspect at the crime scene beyond a reasonable doubt.

Says Robert D. Hall, professor of entomology at the University of Missouri-Columbia, "It's a grisly field . . . but I think the emphasis should be on the wonderful things that can be done with these insects because they're seldom fooled. If you ask them the right questions, they will give you right answers."[10] So no matter how careful murderers are to cover their tracks, criminals can be assured that some creature clues will be found to bear witness against them.

Autopsies

An autopsy is the medical examination of a dead body to determine the cause of death. The medical examiner, who performs the autopsy, looks for wounds and abrasions, such as rope marks on the victim's body, or broken capillaries in the victim's eyes, which indicate strangulation. Photographs and fingerprints are taken of the victim. Physical characteristics are recorded, such as eye and hair color, height, weight, scars, tattoos, number of teeth, and type of dental work on the teeth if any.

The medical examiner also looks at the internal organs to learn how a victim died. The stomach, bladder, and other vital organs are removed for microscopic examination. Contents of the stomach will be examined, and the medical examiner will be able to tell when the victim ate his or her last meal. If poison is suspected, a toxicologist will analyze the blood, urine, stomach, and other body tissues. Poisons such as lead, for example, will show up in the bone tissue, and arsenic will show up in the hair.

In drowning cases, a fine, frothy foam will be found through the respiratory tract, the lungs will be soggy, and the stomach will contain water. Some of the water that enters the lungs when a drowning victim gasps for air will seep into the left side of the heart, thinning the blood there. If the victim was dead before entering the water, the heart blood will not be diluted. This is an important clue in cases where the murderer tries to make his victim's death seem like an accidental drowning.

The Future of Forensics

Current forensic techniques are only a preview of crime-detecting methods that will be available in the twenty-first century. Improved lasers will lift fingerprints from surfaces impossible to get prints from today, such as those found on porous materials like sponges. Police cars will have mini computer terminals to identify the fingerprints of suspects on the spot. Today a partial fingerprint can be fed into a computer, and the name of its owner is printed out. In the future, digitalized technology will allow computers to enhance that partial print into a full-blown fingerprint within seconds.

Another way computers are helping forensic scientists catch criminals is digital image photography, in which images are generated by a series of numbers that can be changed by computer. This has made it possible for the crime lab to fix problems with contrast, brightness, and focus in a photo. Digital image processing is based on technology created by NASA and the Jet Propulsion Laboratory for the space program. The computer divides a photo into more than 300,000 tiny squares called pixels, meaning "picture elements." There are 480 pixels in a row, 640 in a column. Every one of the squares is considered to be a shade of gray, measured on a scale ranging from 0, which is pure black, to 250, which is pure white.[11] Technicians can change the gray scale with the computer, to make parts of a photo lighter or darker and create contrast between different areas. Such contrast makes selected images stand out. Then small details, like license plate numbers of cars in the background, logos on bank robbers' caps and shirts, or writing on documents, become visible.

Digital image processing is also used to remove blurs or correct the focus. What the computer does is push everything in the picture back into focus by squeezing the image together. To do this, the computer needs to find a single point of light on the photo and compress that point of light smaller and smaller. Then the rest of the images in the photo become clearer. After John Hinckley shot former president Ronald Reagan, the lab received a series of badly blurred photos showing someone shooting at the president over the top of a limousine. But the pictures were so blurry it was impossible even to know whether the shooter was a man or woman. The point of light in the photos was a reflection on the limousine's bumper. On the blurred film it appeared to be a line. The computer "knew" that the amount of blur in the picture was equal to the length of that line, so when the line was compressed back into a point, the rest of the images also became sharp. Now it was clear that the shooter was a man, and many of his features could be distinguished.

Computers will continue to change how forensic scientists investigate death. Taken into the autopsy room, computers will allow pathologists to use the three-dimensional X rays of virtual reality technology to analyze and date injuries. Barry Fisher, director of the Scientific Services Bureau for the Los Angeles County Sheriff's Department, predicts computer-aided, virtual reality replicas of crime scenes will become as common a tool as fingerprinting in solving crime. Just like playing a game of virtual reality, in which special gloves and goggles enable players to feel as if they are touching and maneuvering anything in the scene they are "walking through," a computer can be fed the particulars of a case, and a rotating, three-dimensional drawing will reconstruct the crime scene. Then police can "move around" the scene to check eyewitness testimony.[12]

One company used a form of this virtual reality crime scene recreation in the retrial of brothers Lyle and Erik Menendez for the shotgun slayings of their wealthy parents, Jose and Kitty, in their Beverly Hills mansion on August 20, 1989. Lyle was twenty-two, and Erik was nineteen years old at the time. The brothers admitted killing their parents during the first trial, which resulted in a jury deadlocked between first-degree murder and the lesser charge of manslaughter in January 1994. Failure Analysis Associates, named for its original concept of studying the causes of disasters such as car crashes, burned buildings, and sunken ships, offered a courtroom reconstruction of the crime scene in the den, where the murders occurred. Using police photographs and computer-imaging techniques, the jury was literally brought on-scene to witness the final moments of Jose and Kitty Menendez.

Prosecutors hoped to prove the murders were premeditated and were committed so the greedy brothers could get their hands on their parents' fortune, estimated at $14 million. The defense claimed the brothers committed the murders in self-defense after years of sexual and physical abuse, and a mounting fear that their parents planned to kill them. Failure Analysis spent hundreds of hours studying more than eight hundred crime scene and autopsy photos and scanning them into a state-of-the-art digital computer, which printed out the sequence of the gunshots, the number of them, the position of the bodies, and which wounds were inflicted before and after death. This information made the company's experts conclude that the brothers killed their parents execution style, then shot them in the legs to give the killings organized crime overtones.

On March 20, 1996, after the five-month retrial, the jury found Lyle and Erik guilty of first-degree murder with special circumstances, meaning, under California law, murders by lying in wait and multiple murders. The special circumstances leave only two options for sentencing: life in prison without the possibility of parole, or death by execution. The jury decided on the former sentence. Thus, barring any successful appeals, the Menendez brothers will spend the rest of their lives in prison.

The value of all this space age technology, however, will always depend on the person who uses it. When a witness claimed to have seen a car similar to one driven by a dead woman's boyfriend near the woodland where her body was found, Los Angeles County sheriffs confiscated the man's automobile. The criminalist analyzing debris found in the car decided to put a pine needle under his microscope. He noticed a wartlike structure at its tip. Curious, he contacted a botanist, who told him the structure was home to a particular plant mite living only in places at a specific altitude with a southerly exposure. The area in which the body was left matched these specifications. That evidence put the boyfriend at the scene of the crime and helped convict him of murder. As Dr. Barry Fisher said about the case, "Technology helps, but without the skill of examiners, all these whiz-bang innovations would be useless."[13] Anything in the physical universe, absolutely anything, can be evidence in a criminal investigation—from flies on a corpse, to microscopic green flecks in a bottle of aspirin, a bullet embedded in a lamppost, a tiny piece of circuit board found in bombing debris, a thin strand of hair on a suspect's shirt, a carpet fiber on the floor mat of a car, saliva on a stamp, or blood on a knife. Forensic scientists, using all the tools available, will continue to pursue criminals and murderers and bring them to justice, even if only by tiny threads of evidence.

SOURCE NOTES

INTRODUCTION

1. David Fisher, *Hard Evidence: How Detectives Inside the FBI's Sci-Crime Lab Have Helped Solve America's Toughest Cases* (New York: Simon & Schuster, 1995), 17.

2. Susan Goodman, "Body of Evidence: New Forensic Technology Puts Science on the Stand," *Modern Maturity* (October–November 1991), 68.

3. Robert Gardner, *Crime Lab 101: Experimenting With Crime Detection* (Walker, 1992), 8–11.

4. Fisher, *Hard Evidence*, 231.

5. Ibid.

6. Ibid., 231–232.

7. Ibid., 18.

8. Gardner, *Crime Lab 101*, 11.

9. Jon Zonderman, *Beyond the Crime Lab: The New Science of Investigations* (New York: John Wiley and Sons, 1990), 40.

1

1. Fisher, *Hard Evidence*, 14.

2. Ibid., 12–13.

3. Ibid., 13.

4. Ibid., 14–16.

5. Ibid., 19–20.

6. Ibid., 288–289.

7. Ibid., 289–290.

8. Ibid., 295.

9. Ibid., 295–296.

10. James Dickerson, "Murders from the Past," *Omni* (August 1993), 50–82.

11. Fisher, *Hard Evidence*, 21.

2

1. Fisher, *Hard Evidence*, 108.

2. Thomas Lee, *Gene Future: The Promise and Perils of the New Biology* (New York: Plenum, 1993), 125.

3. Fisher, *Hard Evidence*, 148.

4. Ibid., 155–156.

5. Lee, *Gene Future*, 137.

6. Fisher, *Hard Evidence*, 156–157.

7. Joe McGinness, *Fatal Vision* (New York: Putnam, 1983), 448–449.

8. Fisher, *Hard Evidence*, 158.

9. Gardner, *Crime Lab 101*, 60–61.

10. David W. Grogan, "The Lady Vanishes and a Wood Chipper Leaves Just a Shred of Evidence," *People Weekly* (August 1, 1988), 83–88.

11. Mary Curtius, "Davis Convicted of Murdering Polly Klass," *Los Angeles Times* (June 19, 1996), Sec. A20.

12. Ibid., A1, 20, 22.

13. Fisher, *Hard Evidence*, 126–129.

14. Ibid., 130.

15. Zonderman, *Beyond the Crime Lab*, 45–48.

16. Fisher, *Hard Evidence*, 138.

17. Ibid., 134–135.

18. Ibid., 141.

19. Ibid.

3

1. Kevin C. McElfresh, Debbie Vining-Forde, and Ivan Balazs, "DNA-Based Identity Testing in Forensic Science," *Bio Science* (March 1993), 149–153.

2. Ibid.

3. Fisher, *Hard Evidence*, 151–152.

4. McElfresh, Vining-Forde, and Balazs, "DNA-Based Identity Testing," 149–154.

5. John Horgan, "High Profile: The Simpson Case," *Scientific American* (October 1994), 33.

6. Dan Cray, "DNA Fingerprinting," *Time* (May 8, 1994), 24.

7. Ibid.

8. Fisher, *Hard Evidence*, 152.

9. Gardner, *Crime Lab 101*, 64.

10. Michael S. Serrill, "Blood, Sweat, and Tears," *Time* (Europe ed.) (May 15, 1995). (Transmitted through Prodigy on the Internet.)

11. Mike Rodman, "Crime Lab Gets $100,000 for DNA Unit," *Arkansas Gazette*, January 27, 1995, Sec. A, 1.

12. Ibid.

13. Peter J. Neufield and Neville Colman, "When Science Takes the Witness Stand," *Scientific American* (May 1990), 53.

14. Ibid., 46–53.

15. Serrill, "Blood, Sweat, and Tears," *Time* (Europe ed.) (May 15, 1995).

16. Ibid.

4

1. Fisher, *Hard Evidence*, 29–30.

2. Ibid., 228.

3. Ibid.

4. Ibid., 233.

5. John I. Thornton, "New Tools of the Forensic Scientist," *World Book Encyclopedia, Science Yearbook, 1996 Special Report, Technology*, 159–171.

6. Ibid., 169.

7. Ibid., 170.

8. Fisher, *Hard Evidence*, 44–45.

9. Ibid., 131–132.

10. Fisher, *Hard Evidence*, 32–37.

11. Gardner, *Crime Lab 101*, 91–92.

12. Fisher, *Hard Evidence*, 161–163.

13. Ibid., 221.

14. Ibid., 166–171.

15. Robert Sheely, *Police Lab: Using Science to Solve Crimes* (New York: Silver Moon Press, 1993), 36.

16. Fisher, *Hard Evidence*, 224–225.

5

1. Fisher, *Hard Evidence*, 108–111.

2. Sheely, *Police Lab*, 24.

3. Department of Justice, *A Handbook of Forensic Science* (Washington, D.C.: FBI Publication, 1984), 126.

4. Nigel Marven, "Witnesses from the Grave: Turning to Nature for Clues," *PBS Television Nature Series*, March 1995.

5. Fisher, *Hard Evidence*, 63–64.

6. Department of Justice, *Handbook of Forensic Science*, 138.

7. Gardner, *Crime Lab 101*, 25.

8. Fisher, *Hard Evidence*, 101.

9. Ibid., 98–102.

6

1. *New York Times News Service*, August 14, 1995.

2. *New York Times*, February 27, 1996. (Transmitted through Prodigy on the Internet.)

3. Christine Gorman, "How Garden Variety Fertilizer Becomes Killer Bombs," *Time* (May 1, 1995), 20.

4. Ibid.

5. Fisher, *Hard Evidence*, 62.

6. Ibid., 70.

7. Ibid., 76–82.

8. Ibid., 68–74.

9. Michael D. Lemonick, "The Bomb Is in the Mail," *Time* (May 8, 1995), 70ff.

10. Lemonick, "The Bomb Is in the Mail," 70ff.

11. Ronald J. Ostrow and Louis Shahugan, "Family's Agonizing Ordeal of Baring Bomb Suspect Told," *Los Angeles Times* (April 9, 1996), Sec. A, 1,6.

12. K. C. Cole, "3,500 Words Paint a Picture," *Los Angeles Times* (April 11, 1996), Sec. A, 16.

13. Richard C. Paddock, "Taylor-Made Technology Used in Cabin Search," *Los Angeles Times* (April 9, 1996), Sec. A, 1,6.

14. Sherry Stolberg and Mark Gladstone, "Pieces of Wood, A Book, A Letter Mark Long Trail," *Los Angeles Times* (April 5, 1996), Sec. A, 1,17,18.

15. Abigail Goldman, "Unabomber Case Files Trace Trail That Led to Kaczynski," *Los Angeles Times* (June 15, 1996), Sec. A, 29.

16. Stolberg and Gladstone, "Pieces of Wood," 17.

17. Goldman, "Unabomber Case Files," 29.

18. Nancy Gibbs, "Tracking Down the Unabomber," *Time* (April 15, 1996), 45.

19. Stolberg and Gladstone, "Pieces of Wood," 16.

7

1. Vincent Bugliosi, *And the Sea Will Tell* (New York: Norton, 1991), 346.

2. Goodman, "Body of Evidence," 68.

3. Ibid., 69.

4. Patrick Cooke, "Grave Robbers," *Health* (November–December, 1992), 76–82.

5. Horgan, "High Profile: The Simpson Case," 17ff.

6. Marven, "Witnesses from the Grave, " *PBS*, March 1995.

7. Ibid.

8. Ibid.

9. Horgan, "High Profile: The Simpson Case," 17–18.

10. Ibid., 18.

11. Fisher, *Hard Evidence*, 269.

12. Goodman, "Body of Evidence," 68–95.

13. Ibid., 95.

F U R T H E R   R E A D I N G

Bugliosi, Vincent. *And the Sea Will Tell*. New York: Norton, 1991.

Fisher, James. *The Lindbergh Case*. New Brunswick, N.J.: Rutgers University Press, 1987.

Gardner, Robert. *Crime Lab 101: Experimenting With Crime Detection*. New York: Walker, 1992.

Graham, Ian. *Crime Fighting*. Austin: Raintree, 1995.

Herzog, Arthur. *The Woodchipper Murder*. New York: Zebra, 1990.

Maples, William R., and Michael Browning. *Dead Men Do Tell Tales*. New York: Doubleday, 1994.

McGinness, Joe. *Fatal Vision*. New York: Putnam, 1983.

Otfinoski, Steven. *Whodunit? Science Solves the Crime*. New York: W. H. Freeman, 1995.

Sheely, Robert. *Police Lab: Using Science to Solve Crimes*. New York: Silver Moon Press, 1993.

Thomas, Peggy. *Talking Bones: The Science of Forensic Anthropology*. New York: Facts on File, 1995.

I N D E X